Planet Cake
CUPCAKES

Paris Cutler

Illustrations by Margaret Carter

MURDOCH BOOKS

Contents

Cupcake designs

Cut-outs

Faces

Mosaics

Painting & piping

Modelling

Cupcake how-to

Introduction

I have to admit that the cupcake phenomenon took me completely by surprise. When it first started, I felt that cupcakes were just a fad and, although the craze was raging along with alarming speed, my focus was on bigger cakes, more complex cakes or, I guess — if I was being honest — more serious cakes. I saw cupcakes as the poor cousin of conventional cakes and not a celebrated genre unto themselves. Given that this was my standpoint, I am sure you would love to know how I ended up writing a cupcake book. Well, let's just admit, there is much truth to the saying 'pride comes before a fall' and I was to have a very rude awakening about how wrong I was about cupcakes! What made this lesson all the more poignant was that it was delivered to me by a beautiful A-list celebrity.

When I was asked to make Celine Dion's birthday cake, I could not have dreamed of a better opportunity to create a wildly complex and amazing cake than for one of the most talented singers in the world. True to form, we created a cake with just about everything on it: realistic figurines, the Colosseum in Las Vegas, a globe of the world — even Celine's beloved mother made an appearance. It was, without a doubt, one of the best cakes we had ever created and the most technically complex. Luckily for me, Celine thought so too and, as a thank you for her cake, she invited us to her concert and also backstage, where she thanked us personally (we were blown away by her kindness). It was backstage, while I was basking under the incredible graciousness, megawatt smile and attention of Celine Dion, that my cupcake conversion took place. Celine admitted to me that although she thought our cake was by far the most incredible birthday cake she had ever enjoyed, her real love was cupcakes, and did I make any of those?

After recovering from the shock of having our masterpiece trumped by a blob of butter cake in a paper case, I had to seriously re-examine cupcakes. What makes them so charming? My conclusion was that cupcakes inspire two things in people: fantasy and comfort or, put simply, 'magic you can eat'. What makes them even more special is that each one is a little cake, just for you.

When I was approached to write this book, I was a bit apprehensive about what I could bring to cupcakes that had not already been done before. Let's face it, cupcake mania has been around for a while. My first book was a beginner's book and my goal with that book was to introduce people to cake decorating and to reveal how easy cake decorating can be, with the right techniques. The beginner's cupcakes in that book are still a good place to start. I had to think about Planet Cake, my team and our identity, and what our readers and students wanted. I asked a lot of students and the answer was usually the same: they wanted to be inspired.

In this book, I wanted to bring Planet Cake's technical expertise to cupcakes and push the design boundaries to the limit. With the encouragement of our students, I felt it was time to put my foot on the cupcake accelerator. To make the most magical cupcakes that I could dream up, I enlisted the help of my creative partner and the captain of Planet Cake's dream team, Margie Carter; it is her figurine expertise that allows me to bring my fantasies for this book alive.

I know you will all have the same experience as I have had with cupcakes; they are powerful little things and can take you places you never thought possible. I call this phenomenon the 'power of the cupcake' and I wish I had known what I know now when I met Celine — but maybe she will read the book!

How to use this book

This book is divided into two sections. In the first part, you will find a series of gorgeous cupcakes and step-by-step instructions for making them. Grouped into chapters according to the techniques required to make them, they are also arranged roughly in order of difficulty, from the easiest to the most challenging. If you are new to cake decorating, we suggest you start with one of the easier designs and move gradually on to the more difficult techniques, once you start to feel confident. But that doesn't mean you can't have a go at the more difficult cupcakes — they just require a little more time and patience.

The second section of the book contains everything you need to know about making and decorating the cupcakes in this book, from equipment, materials and basic recipes to techniques, tips and templates. There's also a handy troubleshooting section and glossary.

I cannot emphasise enough how important it is to prepare your work space. Making cupcakes is, above all, some time out for you to enjoy yourself. Therefore, before you start decorating put on some of your favourite music, take the phone off the hook, make sure you have everything you require including room in your freezer (if necessary), bench space, equipment and peace and quiet. Re-read your instructions and smile! Remember that the only way to improve is with practice, so take your time and enjoy the journey. A cupcake made with love will always be a success with your audience.

Essential planning and preparation

Design (1 month prior)

All the cupcake designs in this book can be tailored to your own specific needs. We have tried to teach you decorating techniques that can be easily adapted to other subjects. Obviously, the easiest thing to change is the colour palette. However, you can also change the decoration detail, mixing and matching elements of a design so it suits your occasion exactly. The best ideas for cake designs, in my opinion, come from children's books and colouring books, cartoons, food packaging, toys, stationery, fabrics and even buttons; all these have been used to design the cupcakes in this book and will always be great sources of design inspiration. If you are using a stand or displaying your cupcakes on a board, do not ignore this element in the design process. Display stands and boards that maintain the cupcake story or theme will transform your cupcakes into something really special.

Planning (2 weeks prior)

You should be prepared at least 2 weeks in advance if you want to avoid stress. Making and decorating cakes always takes longer than you think. For an enjoyable experience, it is important to be as organised as possible. If you are making cupcakes for a special event, make sure you have all the materials and equipment necessary and are happy with your chosen design. If you are planning on making figurines, make these as far in advance as possible; they will take longer than you imagine, but can be stored almost indefinitely in the right conditions, so you might as well make them early on. If you are making or using a stand, now is the time to organise it. It is also important to remember that with specialist hobbies, some products might need to be ordered in advance.

Timing guideline

At Planet Cake, we work to the following timing guideline when covering our cupcakes.

1 Bake your cupcakes and allow to cool (at least 30 minutes). They can be frozen at this stage.

2 Trim and ganache your cupcakes.

3 Set aside for 4 hours or until the ganache is firm to the touch.

4 Cover with fondant icing and decorate.

Tip

You will learn quickly not to cut corners; cupcakes that are not allowed to cool or ganache that has not set will make poor foundations and the result will be wonky decorating and an exasperating experience.

Getting cupcakes started

Choose the cupcakes you want to make and read the step-by-step instructions. You should also have a look at the checklist of techniques that are used for your chosen cupcakes. When you need to know more, flip to the how-to section (page 198) to find an explanation of all the techniques and tips you'll need, to make your perfect cupcake. If you have never used a particular technique before, allow yourself some time to practise, so that you can be confident about getting it right on the actual cupcakes.

Every project begins with a number of pre-ganached cupcakes, so check the number of cakes you will need for the particular project, then follow the recipes for baking and ganaching that number of cupcakes.

When you're ready to begin decorating, gather all your supplies and follow the steps and diagrams, one after the other, until you're done.

FAQs

What size cupcakes are you using in the book?

All of the cupcakes in the book have a 7 cm (2¾ in) diameter top: at Planet Cake this is the standard cupcake size. You can adjust the instructions according to different sizes if you want to, based on this standard size.

Can I use these designs for mini cupcakes?

We find mini cupcakes very difficult to decorate and cover with rolled fondant icing; however, it is not impossible, just more challenging, as everything is smaller.

What is the best way to transport cupcakes?

At Planet Cake, we attach our cupcakes to an iced display board with a small amount of icing or ganache underneath each one. This stops them from moving. Alternatively, you can move them in a cupcake box or in a cupcake carrier. The rule is to keep them firm and stable, but not too close together.

What is the best way to store cupcakes?

Do not refrigerate cupcakes covered with fondant icing; they will sweat and be ruined. Keep them cool (gentle air conditioning is best), and away from bright light (many colours will fade in the light). Cardboard cake boxes are good for storing iced and decorated cupcakes as they aren't airtight and they will protect them from the light. Alternatively, store iced cupcakes in a container draped with a cloth to keep out the light.

Cupcake
designs

Cut-outs

This is perhaps the easiest cupcake-decorating technique, so it's a great place to start your cupcake-decorating adventures. Use paper templates to cut simple shapes from rolled icing and use the shapes to decorate your cupcakes. Start with a simple design until you feel confident, and then — the sky's the limit!

Parachute rainbows

One of the reasons I love cupcakes is that they can be created simply to make someone happy — and they don't have to wait for a celebratory event. This cupcake story is a classic example of cupcakes designed to bring joy. The parachute rainbows design is very easy to replicate and can, with a bit of imagination, be personalised.

Materials

6 ganached cupcakes
100 ml (3½ fl oz) syrup
Cornflour in shaker
500 g (1 lb 2 oz) fondant icing
Colour paste: red, black,
    brown, blue, yellow,
    purple, green, orange
Cake-decorating alcohol
White and black royal icing
Pink and red petal dust

Equipment

2B pencil and tracing paper
Large and small rolling pins
Cranked palette knife
Small sharp kitchen knife
Flexi-smoother
Pastry brush
Ruler
Balling tool
Frilling tool
Fine paintbrushes
Piping bag
No. 1, No. 2 and No. 3 piping tips
Circle cutters
50 cm (20 in) square cake board
    (optional)

Techniques checklist

Recipes (page 204)
Ganaching cupcakes (page 208)
Making a template (page 221)
Colouring fondant icing
    (page 210)
Skin-coloured icing (page 211)
Red and black icing (page 211)
Covering cupcakes (page 209)
Transferring a template
    (page 221)
Edible painting and colour wash
    (page 213)
Blush (page 214)
Piping with royal icing
    (page 217)

Step-by-step

1 Make templates. Trace the parachute man, parachute and aeroplane outlines from pages 12 and 13 to make the templates.

2 Colour fondant icing. Mix the colours the day before if possible, to make the intense colours easier to work with. You will require about 250 g (9 oz) bright blue icing for the covers, as well as small amounts of red, orange, yellow, green, purple, black, grey and white, and a very small amount of skin-coloured icing.

3 Cover cupcakes. Allowing about 40 g (1½ oz) per cupcake, roll bright blue icing to 3 mm (⅛ in) thick and cover your ganached cupcakes.

4 Decorate cupcakes.

CLOUDS Roll out white icing to 3 mm (⅛ in) thick. Using a small sharp knife, cut out two freehand cloud shapes. Don't worry if they're a bit wonky — clouds are not regular. Gently smooth the edges with your finger.

Put a 7 cm (2¾ in) cutter over a cloud to give an idea of how it will look on the cupcake. Move the cutter to where you want the edge of the cloud to be, then press to cut the curved edge. Stick cloud onto cupcake with a dab of water. Repeat with the remaining cloud.

Roll out white icing to 3 mm (⅛ in) thick and cut out cloud shapes, then smooth edges.

Place a 7 cm (2¾ in) circle cutter over cloud and cut.

Attach cloud to cupcake.

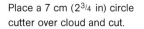

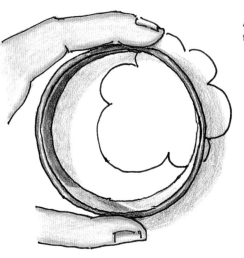

Pipe V-shaped birds, tapering each line from thicker at the bottom to thin at the top.

BIRDS The birds are piped onto the cupcake, using a black royal icing and a No. 2 piping tip. If you're nervous about piping, practise first on a piece of scrap icing, or on your work surface. Squeeze the icing from the tip onto the surface. Pull the tip away from the starting point in a small arc, using less pressure as you pull. This will taper the royal icing to a point as you draw it away. Repeat this action at a V-angle from the first line of piping, as shown. And there you have it — a bird in flight!

RAINBOW If necessary, use a 2B pencil to lightly sketch in the arc of the rainbow onto the cover of the cupcake with the other cloud. Roll red, orange, yellow, green and purple icing to 2–3 mm ($1/16$–$1/8$ in) thick and, using a ruler, cut strips, about 6 mm ($1/4$ in) wide and about 7 cm ($2\,3/4$ in) long, for each cupcake. Stick the strips on the cupcake, in rainbow order, with a small dab of water. Place the end of each strip against the edge of the cloud first, cutting it at an angle, if necessary, for a neat fit. Gently curve the strip across the cupcake in an arc and trim the excess at the outer edge.

To continue the rainbow's arc onto another cake, lightly sketch in the curve with a pencil, and then apply the strips as before.

SUN Roll out yellow icing to 3 mm ($1/8$ in) thick and, using a circle cutter approximately 3.5 cm ($1\,3/8$ in) in diameter, cut out the centre of the sun. Apply to a cupcake with a dab of water. From the rest of the icing, use a sharp knife to cut thin strips of varying lengths, for the sun's rays, as shown. Attach the rays, one by one, trimming them to fit.

Attach with a dab of water.

Trim ends neatly to fit against edge of cloud.

Draw light pencil lines as a guide for rainbow.

Cut strips of fondant for rainbow.

Use a pencil to continue rainbow arc from one cake to another.

Roll yellow icing to 3 mm ($1/8$ in) thick.

Trim rays to fit and apply around sun with a dab of water.

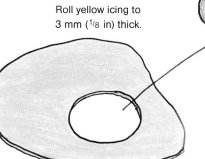

Cut out a circle for the sun, smooth edges and place on cupcake.

Cut thin strips from icing for sun's rays.

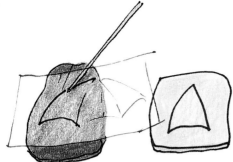

Transfer parachute segments onto coloured icing and cut out.

Transfer parachute man to grey icing, then cut out.

PARACHUTE MAN Roll yellow, red and green icing to 3 mm (1/8 in) thick and, using the template, transfer each of the parachute segments to a different coloured icing.

Cut out the pieces with a sharp knife and place them back together on a cupcake with a dab of water.

For the little man, roll out grey icing thinly and, using the template, cut out the parachute suit and adhere to the cupcake with a dab of water. Indent the centre of the helmet with a balling tool, then flatten a small ball of skin-coloured icing and stick it into the indent. Roll two tiny, rice-grain-sized balls each of black and skin-coloured icing and flatten them slightly for the shoes and hands, respectively. Mark fingers on the hands with the back of a knife. Stick the pieces on the cupcake with a dab of water.

Mix black colour paste and alcohol and paint the suit details and face. Rub a little petal dust into the cheeks with a dry paintbrush. Using a No. 1 piping tip and black royal icing, pipe fine lines from the man's hands to the parachute.

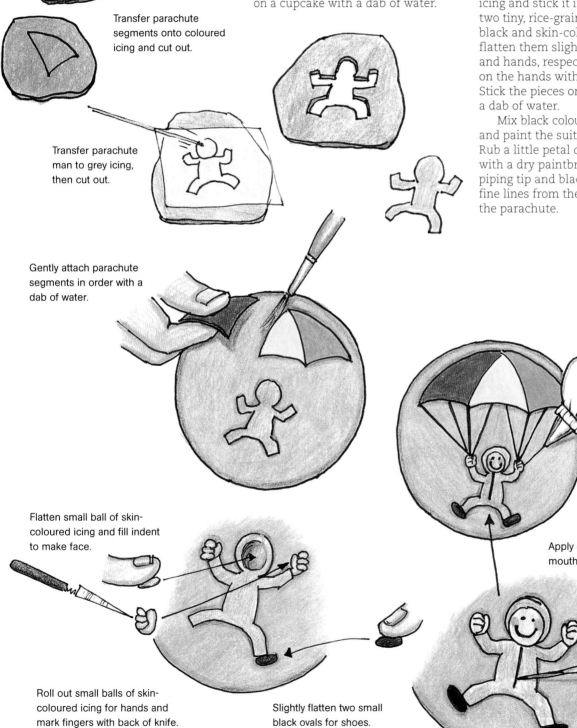

Gently attach parachute segments in order with a dab of water.

Pipe parachute lines using a No. 1 tip.

Flatten small ball of skin-coloured icing and fill indent to make face.

Apply cheek blush, paint eyes, mouth and jumpsuit details.

Roll out small balls of skin-coloured icing for hands and mark fingers with back of knife.

Slightly flatten two small black ovals for shoes.

AEROPLANE Roll out some orange icing (or the colour of your choice) to 3 mm (⅛ in) thick and, using the template, cut out the body of the plane and the wings with a sharp kitchen knife. Indent the windscreen with a frilling tool, then roll and cut a tiny, thin windscreen of white icing, and stick it into the indent, as shown. Mix red colour paste and alcohol and paint the wings and tail if desired.

Adhere the completed plane to the top of a cupcake with water.

Use a 2B pencil to lightly sketch in the heart shape of the plane's vapour trail. Using a No. 3 piping tip and white royal icing, pipe the heart shape in a slightly wiggly line, using more pressure at the thickest part of the line and less pressure as you taper off to the final dots at the tip of the heart.

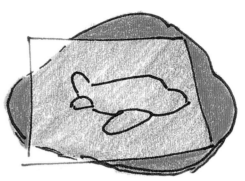

Transfer and cut out aeroplane.

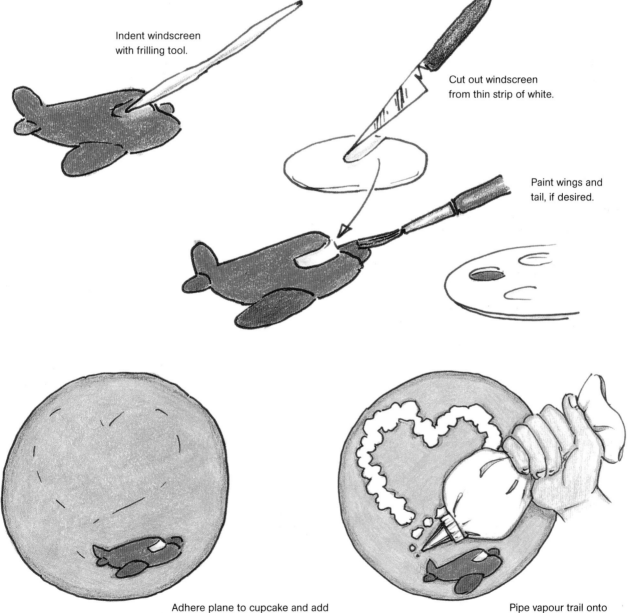

Indent windscreen with frilling tool.

Cut out windscreen from thin strip of white.

Paint wings and tail, if desired.

Adhere plane to cupcake and add light pencil lines to guide you when piping vapour trail.

Pipe vapour trail onto cupcake, using a No. 3 tip.

Spaceman

How could a store like Planet Cake pass up the opportunity for a space story? Please feel free to play with our design — you can subtract or add as many elements as you desire and quite easily personalise the design for the birthday boy or girl. The techniques required are simple to master and you should enjoy making this design.

Materials

6 ganached cupcakes
100 ml (3½ fl oz) syrup
Cornflour in shaker
500 g (1 lb 2 oz) fondant icing
Colour paste: red, blue, green,
    yellow, black, brown, orange
Red and pink petal dust
Edible silver dust
Cake-decorating alcohol
Airbrush colour of your choice

Equipment

Large and small rolling pins
Cranked palette knife
Small sharp kitchen knife
Tiny round cutter (optional)
Flexi-smoother
Pastry brush
Frilling tool
Small balling tool
Fine paintbrush
Circle cutters
Tiny star cutter (optional)
No. 4 piping tip
Airbrush machine
50 cm (20 in) square cake board
    (optional)

Techniques checklist

Step-by-step

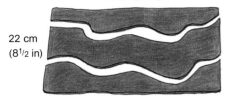

30 cm (12 in)

22 cm
(8½ in)

Roll out dark blue icing
and cut out wavy strips.

Roll out light blue icing and use
dark blue waves as templates to
cut Milky Way strips.

1 Make templates. Trace the outlines for the spaceman and spaceships from pages 20 and 21 to make templates.

2 Colour fondant icing. Mix the colours the day before if possible, to make the intense colours easier to work with. You will require about 200 g (7 oz) dark blue icing and about 120 g (4¼ oz) light blue for the Milky Way covers, as well as small amounts of white, orange, red, green, pale yellow, brown, grey and a tiny amount of skin-coloured icing, for the decorations. For the planets, you will need to marble some of these colours together.

3 Cover cupcakes. To make the Milky Way covers, roll out dark blue icing into a 3 mm (⅛ in) thick rectangle about 22 x 30 cm (8½ x 12 in). Using a small sharp knife, cut away two narrow, wavy strips of icing, as shown. Roll out light blue icing to a similar length and gently lay the dark blue cut-out wavy strips on top. Use them as a template to cut identical wavy strips from the light blue icing. Using a paintbrush, dab water along the cut edges of the dark blue base colour and insert the light blue strips into the gaps. Smooth over the top of the icing with a flexi-smoother.

Now centre a 7 cm (2¾ in) cutter over the area you wish to cut and cut out six covers, each with a Milky Way stripe running across it. Smooth the covers onto the ganached cupcakes.

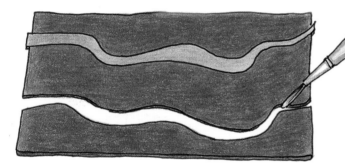

Insert wavy strips into gaps.

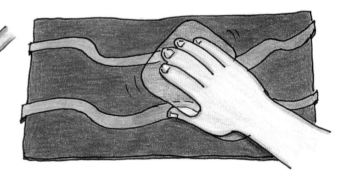

Smooth in place with a flexi-smoother.

Cut covers with a 7 cm (2¾ in) cutter.

Cover cupcakes
and smooth.

4 Decorate cupcakes.

Spaceman cake

SPACEMAN Roll out a small amount of white icing to 3 mm ($\frac{1}{8}$ in) thick and, using the template, cut out a spaceman. Smooth the edges with your fingertip. Use a tiny round cutter or a piping tip to cut a hole for the face. Using the same cutter, cut a thin round of skin-coloured icing for the face and attach it in the hole. Cut the badge and panel details from coloured icing and adhere to the spaceman, using the photograph (page 26) and diagrams as a guide. Roll small pieces of orange icing into strips and attach three to each knee and elbow area. Adhere the spaceman to the cake with a little water. Cut out a tiny fringe of hair, mark it with the frilling tool and adhere to the face. Add rosy cheeks using petal dust applied with a dry paintbrush and paint in face details using black colour paste mixed with alcohol. Cut and adhere narrow strips of grey icing for the belt and lifeline.

Roll white icing for spaceman. Trace, cut out and smooth edges.

Cut out and attach:

A skin-coloured face.

Astronaut badge.

Yellow panel.

Add planet.

Cut out, mark and attach hair.

Paint eyes and mouth.

Add cheek blush.

Paint smaller stars in silver. Attach larger stars.

Cut out and attach belt and lifeline.

PLANET Roll out and cut a small circle of marbled icing for the planet and adhere to the cake. Using a tiny star cutter or working freehand, cut and attach small pale yellow stars. Paint tiny dots and additional twinkling stars in various sizes with silver dust mixed with alcohol.

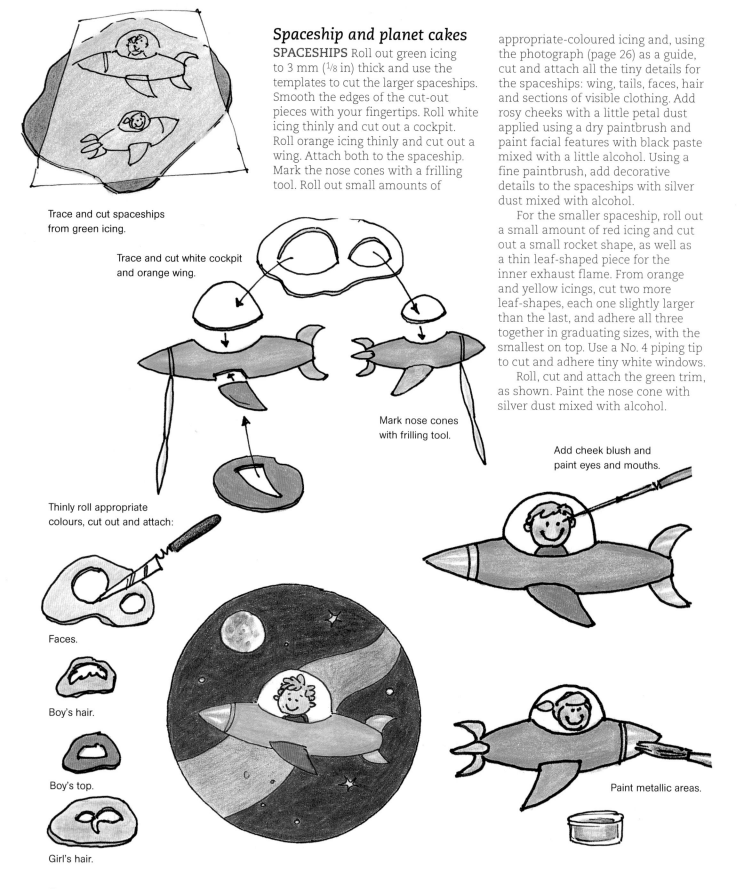

Spaceship and planet cakes

SPACESHIPS Roll out green icing to 3 mm (1/8 in) thick and use the templates to cut the larger spaceships. Smooth the edges of the cut-out pieces with your fingertips. Roll white icing thinly and cut out a cockpit. Roll orange icing thinly and cut out a wing. Attach both to the spaceship. Mark the nose cones with a frilling tool. Roll out small amounts of appropriate-coloured icing and, using the photograph (page 26) as a guide, cut and attach all the tiny details for the spaceships: wing, tails, faces, hair and sections of visible clothing. Add rosy cheeks with a little petal dust applied using a dry paintbrush and paint facial features with black paste mixed with a little alcohol. Using a fine paintbrush, add decorative details to the spaceships with silver dust mixed with alcohol.

For the smaller spaceship, roll out a small amount of red icing and cut out a small rocket shape, as well as a thin leaf-shaped piece for the inner exhaust flame. From orange and yellow icings, cut two more leaf-shapes, each one slightly larger than the last, and adhere all three together in graduating sizes, with the smallest on top. Use a No. 4 piping tip to cut and adhere tiny white windows.

Roll, cut and attach the green trim, as shown. Paint the nose cone with silver dust mixed with alcohol.

Trace and cut spaceships from green icing.

Trace and cut white cockpit and orange wing.

Mark nose cones with frilling tool.

Thinly roll appropriate colours, cut out and attach:

Faces.

Boy's hair.

Boy's top.

Girl's hair.

Add cheek blush and paint eyes and mouths.

Paint metallic areas.

PLANETS AND MOON Roll out balls of assorted marbled colours and white icing (for the moon) and use small round cutters in various sizes up to about 3 cm (1¼ in) to cut circles. Round the edges gently with your fingertips. Using the photograph as a guide, cut a ring for Saturn from pale yellow icing, and adhere to the surface of the planet. Mark craters in the surface of one planet and the moon with frilling and balling tools. Fill the airbrush with alcohol and a drop or two of desired shading colour. Airbrush the moon, applying the paint at an angle from the side to accentuate the craters. Repeat with desired colours for cratered planet.

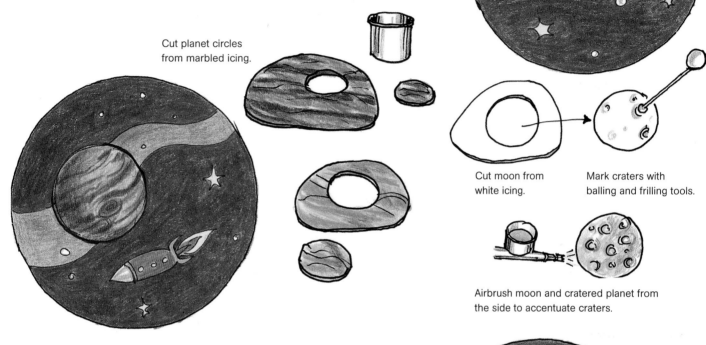

Cut planet circles from marbled icing.

Cut moon from white icing.

Mark craters with balling and frilling tools.

Airbrush moon and cratered planet from the side to accentuate craters.

Cut smaller rocket and exhaust flame from red icing.

Cut larger exhaust shapes and stick all 3 together.

Cut white windows with No. 4 piping tip.

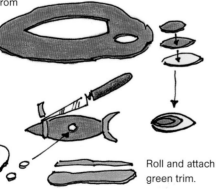

Roll and attach green trim.

Finish with cut-out stars and silver-painted stars.

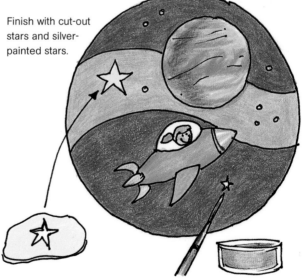

Paint nose cone silver.

FINISHING Apply all the elements to the cupcakes with a dab of water. Finish each cake as for the spaceman cake, with small cut-out stars and painted twinkling silver stars, placed at random.

Faces

A face is round and so is a cupcake — the two are natural partners. Starting with a basic covered cupcake, you can add details to your heart's content, creating a whole cast of gorgeous characters, from babies to monsters — all almost too good to eat!

Flying hearts

Every time one of my friends falls in love or has their heart broken, I try to find the right gift to offer joy or sympathy. This was the idea behind these flying hearts: simple to make, and inspiring to receive.

Materials

6 ganached cupcakes
100 ml (3½ fl oz) syrup
Cornflour in shaker
750 g (1 lb 10 oz) fondant icing
Colour paste: red, pink,
    black, blue
Cake-decorating alcohol
Tylose powder
Airbrush colour: pink, red and
    blue (optional)
Small amount white royal
    icing (optional)

Equipment

2B pencil, fine tip pen, A3 paper
    and tracing paper
Large and small rolling pins
Cranked palette knife
Small sharp kitchen knife
Flexi-smoother
Pastry brush
Frilling tool
Fine paintbrush
Piping bag and No. 2 piping tip
    (optional)
Circle cutters
6.5 cm (2½ in) heart cutter
    (or template)
22-gauge florist's wire or
    dried spaghetti
Airbrush machine (optional)
50 cm (20 in) square cake board
    (optional)

Techniques checklist

Recipes (page 204)
Ganaching cupcakes (page 208)
Making a template (page 221)
Colouring fondant icing
    (page 210)
Red and black icing (page 211)
Covering cupcakes (page 209)
Transferring a template
    (page 221)
Edible painting and colour wash
    (page 213)
Piping with royal icing
    (page 217)
Airbrushing (optional, page 216)

Step-by-step

1 Make templates. Trace outlines of wings and hearts from pages 30 and 31 to make templates.

2 Colour fondant icing. Mix the colours the day before if possible, to make intense colours easier to work with. You will need about 120 g (4¼ oz) each of deep blue and black for covers, 120 g (4¼ oz) each of deep pink and red for hearts and 250 g (9 oz) white for wings.

3 Wings (prepare the day before). Mix a little Tylose powder (see Figurine Modelling, page 218) into the white icing and roll to 3 mm (⅛ in) thickness. Using your wing templates, cut out two wings for each cupcake. Cover with plastic wrap to prevent drying out. Cut 22-gauge wire or spaghetti into 5 cm (2 in) lengths and insert the end into the wing from the bottom, leaving about 2.5 cm (1 in) exposed to insert into the cupcake. Use a frilling tool to make indents in the wings, as shown. Leave uncovered for 24 hours, or longer, to dry. For extra impact, dry the tips of the wing over a pen for a curled effect. Mix a little blue colour paste with alcohol and brush into the indents to add shading and depth, or use an airbrush to add a pale blue tint.

4 Cover cupcakes. Cover three of the ganached cupcakes in black icing and the other three in deep blue icing, allowing about 40 g (1½ oz) per cake.

Transfer wing templates onto rolled-out white icing, and cut out two wings for each cupcake. Keep covered to prevent them drying out.

Insert wire into each wing, then use frilling tool to make indents.

Lightly airbrush or paint pale blue contrast on wings and allow to dry.

Use either a cutter or
a template to cut out
heart shapes.

If desired, airbrush around the
edges of the hearts before
placing on covered cupcakes,
using pink colour on pink hearts,
red colour on red hearts.

5 Decorate cupcakes.

HEARTS Roll out red and deep pink icing to about 4 mm ($^1/_3$ in) thick. Use a heart cutter or template to cut out a heart for each cake. Remember to keep the icing covered at all times so it does not dry out. With warm fingers, rub the edges of each heart until they are bevelled; the sides of the hearts should be gently rounded. If desired, airbrush around the edges of the hearts before placing them on the covered cupcakes with a dab of water, using pink colour on pink hearts and red colour on red hearts.

FACES With a fine paintbrush, paint the face details with black colour paste mixed with alcohol, either tracing the outlines or freehand, using the photographs as a guide.

6 Attach wings. Insert the extending wire into the cupcake top, either into or just below the icing. If you are having trouble attaching the wings, you can pipe a small amount of white royal icing onto the edge of the cover where the wing meets the cupcake before inserting the wires into the cake to serve.

Tip

Practise cutting your shapes from a piece of rolled-out icing before you begin the real thing.

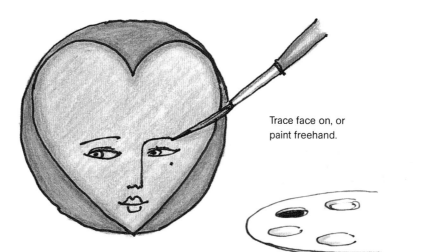

Trace face on, or
paint freehand.

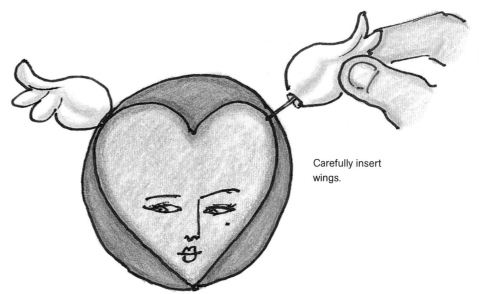

Carefully insert
wings.

Baby suits

Our baby cupcakes always cause a sensation and they never fail to be the most popular request at our shows and demonstrations. The only problem with making these designs is that you will be asked to make them again and again.

Materials

6 ganached cupcakes
100 ml (3½ fl oz) syrup
Cornflour in shaker
750 g (1 lb 10 oz) fondant icing
Colour paste: red, yellow, brown,
   orange, black, pink,
   white-white
Cake-decorating alcohol
Red and pink petal dust
Piping gel
Dried spaghetti

Equipment

Large and small rolling pins
Cranked palette knife
Small sharp kitchen knife
Flexi-smoother
Pastry brush
Frilling tool
Fine and medium paintbrushes
Circle cutters
50 cm (20 in) square cake board
   (optional)

Techniques checklist

Recipes (page 204)
Ganaching cupcakes (page 208)
Colouring fondant icing
   (page 210)
Red and black icing (page 211)
Skin-coloured icing (page 211)
Covering cupcakes (page 209)
Eyes (page 215)
Blush (page 214)
Gelling (page 213)

Step-by-step

1 Colour fondant icing. Mix colours the day before if possible, to make intense colours easier to work with. You will need about 40 g (1½ oz) icing for the cover of each cupcake (pink skin, olive skin and dark skin), as well as about 80 g (2¾ oz) white, and 40 g (1½ oz) each of yellow, orange, grey and brown, for the animal suits, and small amounts of yellow, pink, pale pink, black, light brown and dark brown for the decorations, as shown.

2 Cover cupcakes. It is best to cover and complete each different type of cake individually, rather than covering them all at once. Roll out 40 g (1½ oz) balls of the skin-coloured icing of your choice to 3 mm (⅛ in) thick and cover the ganached cupcakes.

3 Decorate cupcakes.

BASIC BABY SUIT First, work out where the animal suit will cover the baby's head, then study the photograph and diagrams. Note that babies' faces usually occupy the bottom quarter of their head. Each little suit is made in the same basic way, then customised according to the animal. For each suit, you need to roll and cut out a 3 mm (⅛ in) thick circle of the appropriate coloured icing (white for panda and bunny, brown for puppy, yellow for kitten, grey for mouse and orange for tiger), using a circle cutter one size bigger than the one used for the face. Remove one-third of the circle, using the same cutter, and place the remaining two-thirds on the cupcake with a dab of water.

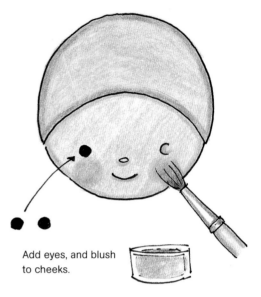

Add eyes, and blush to cheeks.

BASIC BABY FACE While the cover icing is still soft, indent the eye sockets and mouths with a frilling tool. For the panda eyes, make two shallow indents. For the nose, roll a tiny ball of the appropriate skin-coloured icing and stick it in the bottom quarter of the face, between the eyes, with a dab of water.

For the round eyes, roll two small black balls and insert into the eye sockets with a dab of water.

Mix red and pink petal dust to the desired colour and rub it onto the cheeks with a dry paintbrush.

Ears

The ears are all constructed and attached to the cupcake in the same basic way, with differences in shape and colour for each animal (see individual details, opposite). Except for the puppy, all the ears have a supporting piece of spaghetti inserted into them from the bottom edge, leaving about 3 cm (1¼ in) extending for insertion into the cake.

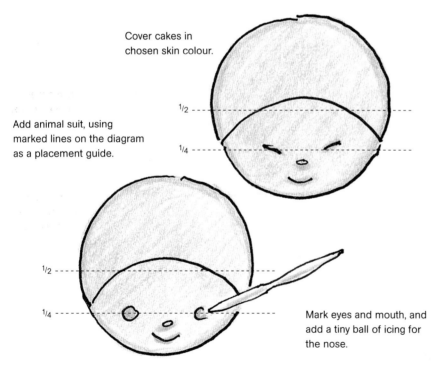

Cover cakes in chosen skin colour.

Add animal suit, using marked lines on the diagram as a placement guide.

½

¼

Mark eyes and mouth, and add a tiny ball of icing for the nose.

½

¼

Tip

The colour of the babies' little noses can be changed to match the animals, for example, a brown nose for the puppy suit or a black nose for the panda suit.

BUNNY, MOUSE, PANDA AND PUPPY EARS

Roll out the appropriate amount of the correct colour for each animal (two grape-sized pieces for the bunny and mouse, two large grape-sized pieces for the puppy, and two large pea-sized pieces for the panda). Press the icing with your finger to flatten it to about 3 mm (1/8 in) thick and round the edges gently into an ear shape, using the diagram as a guide.

For the inner ear (except for the puppy and the panda), roll out a slightly smaller ball of icing in the appropriate colour and press and smooth it into a thinner, smaller version of the outer ear. Attach the inner ear to the outer ear with a dab of water, then insert a piece of spaghetti, where needed.

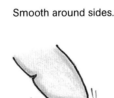

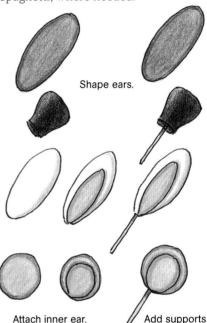

Roll out icing for each ear.

Press down to about 3 mm (1/8 in) thick.

Smooth around sides.

Roll out inner ear colour.

Press down to about 2 mm (1/16 in) thick.

Smooth around sides.

Shape ears.

Attach inner ear.

Add supports where needed.

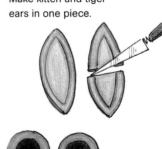

Make kitten and tiger ears in one piece.

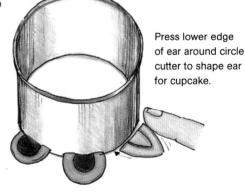

Press lower edge of ear around circle cutter to shape ear for cupcake.

Cut each piece in half to make 2 ears.

KITTEN AND TIGER EARS

You can make these in one piece, because they are smaller. Take a large grape-sized piece of icing (orange for the tiger; yellow for the kitten) and press it into a 3 mm (1/8 in) thick circle or leaf shape (as appropriate), with your fingers, as shown. Fashion a smaller, thinner inner ear in the same way (black for tiger; pink for kitten) and adhere it with a dab of water to the outer ear shape. Cut each shape in half across the middle, giving two

matching ears, then press the lower edge of each ear against the edge of the round cutter used for the baby suit — this makes a gently curved edge to fit the shape of the cupcake. Carefully insert spaghetti supports.

Insert supports.

KITTEN AND TIGER STRIPES
Roll out a small amount of icing (orange for the kitten; black for the tiger) into a narrow strip, about 2 mm ($^1/_{16}$ in) thick and, using the photograph as a guide, cut narrow triangles in varying sizes. Adhere them to the cupcakes, as shown, with a dab of water on each.

Roll out kitten and tiger stripe colours to about 2 mm ($^1/_{16}$ in) thick. Cut into triangle segments and adhere to baby suits.

KISS CURL Roll out a small sausage of icing and taper it at one end to a point. Press gently with your finger to flatten the end and mark with a frilling tool to give the appearance of hair. Gently twist the pointy end into a little curl, then attach the piece to the baby's face or suit with a dab of water.

FRINGE Roll out a small piece of icing thinly and use a circle cutter to cut the desired basic shape. Cut away small triangular sections of icing to give a jagged hairline, then mark hair with a frilling tool and attach the piece to the baby with a dab of water.

Use circle cutter to make fringe shapes.

Roll out tapered icing for hair and press end flattish.

Mark with frilling tool.

Cut out triangles and mark hair.

Cut off excess and mark hair. Attach to puppy.

Attach to panda.

Curl end and attach to mouse or kitten.

TIGHTLY CURLED HAIR Roll several tiny balls of black icing and attach to the face and tiger suit in a tight bunch with water.

Roll out black icing balls and attach to tiger.

FINISHING Dab some water onto the icing where you want to place the ears and insert the extending end of the spaghetti into the cupcake. For the puppy, adhere the ears to the suit, as shown, with a dab of water. Mix black or brown colour paste with alcohol and paint in the eyebrows, mouth indents and freckles with a fine paintbrush.

For the eyes on the baby panda, carefully paint in the eye indents on either side of the little nose.

For the puppy's tongue, roll a tiny oval-shaped piece of red icing and mark the centre indent with a frilling tool. Cut one end off straight and attach the tongue with a dab of water, placing the straight end in the mouth indent. Paint all the round eyes and the puppy's tongue with piping gel to make them shine, and allow to dry. Finish the eyes with white-white colour paste highlights.

Insert ears.

Use a dab of water to adhere puppy ears.

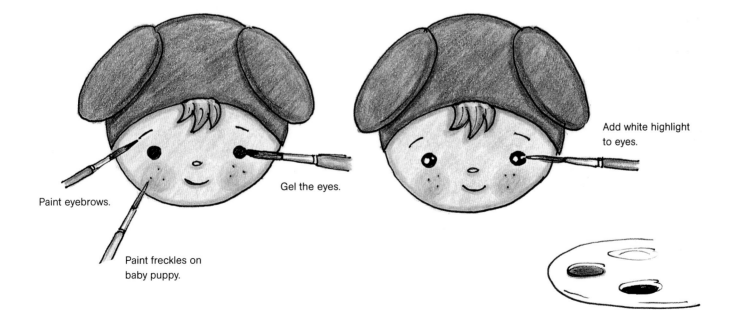

Paint eyebrows.

Paint freckles on baby puppy.

Gel the eyes.

Add white highlight to eyes.

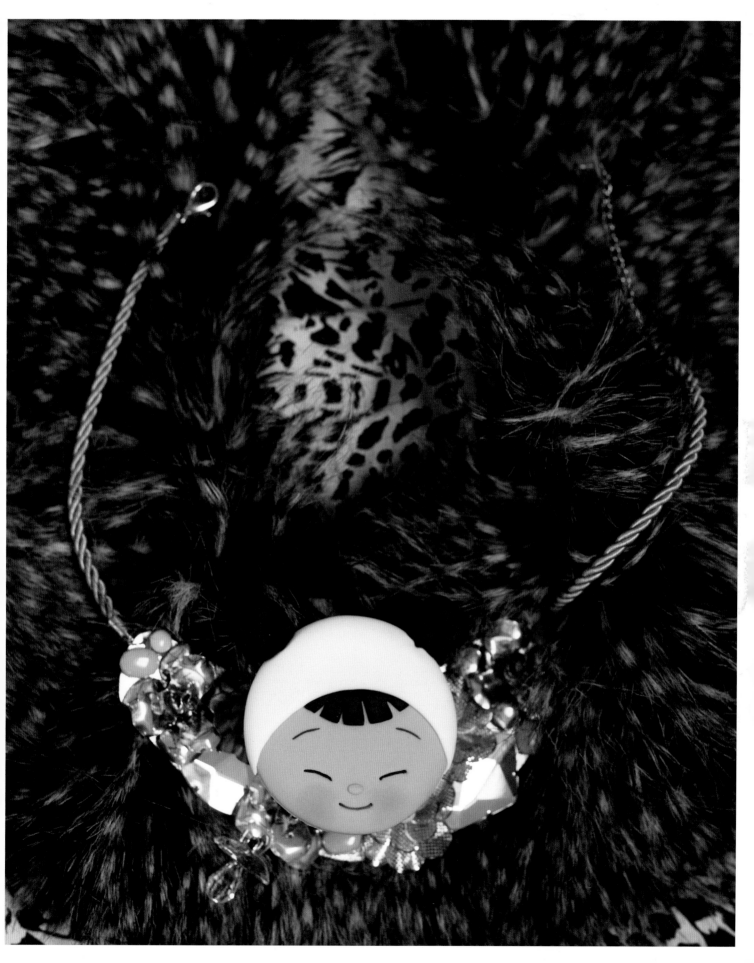

Santa's crew

Merry Christmas! These cupcakes look just as good if you only choose one design. They make fantastic Christmas gifts when boxed in a clear box and tied with a decorative bow.

Materials

5 ganached cupcakes
100 ml (3½ fl oz) syrup
Cornflour in shaker
750 g (1 lb 10 oz) fondant icing
Colour paste: red, yellow,
    brown, black, green, pink,
    white-white
Cake-decorating alcohol
Red and pink petal dust
Piping gel
Dried spaghetti

Equipment

Large and small rolling pins
Cranked palette knife
Small sharp kitchen knife
Flexi-smoother
Pastry brush
Frilling tool
Fine and medium paintbrushes
Circle cutters
22-gauge florist's wire (or twigs),
    for antlers
Brown florist's tape
Dried Spaghetti
Glue gun
50 cm (20 in) square cake board
    (optional)

Techniques checklist

Recipes (page 204)
Ganaching cupcakes (page 208)
Colouring fondant icing
    (page 210)
Skin-coloured icing (page 211)
Red and black icing (page 211)
Covering cupcakes (page 209)
Edible painting and colour wash
    (page 213)
Eyes (page 215)
Blush (page 214)
Gelling (page 213)

Step-by-step

1 Make fondant icing. Mix the colours the day before if possible, to make intense colours easier to work with. You will need about 200 g (7 oz) pink-skin-coloured icing and 50 g (1¾ oz) brown, for the covers and ears, as well as about 100 g (3½ oz) each of red and white, 150 g (5½ oz) light green and small amounts of yellow, dark green, black, pink and light brown icing.

2 Cover cupcakes. It is best to cover and complete each different type of cake individually, rather than covering them all at once. Allow about 40 g (1½ oz) icing per cupcake, using skin-coloured icing for Santa and elves and brown icing for Rudolph.

Bend wire to desired shape and glue-gun antler branches to main wire shape.

Bind antlers with brown florist's tape.

ANTLERS Bend two pieces of 22-gauge wire into a slightly curved shape. Cut smaller pieces of wire for the antler branches and glue-gun them to the antler wires, as shown. Wrap each antler neatly with brown florist's tape, then insert the antlers into the top of Rudolph's head, between the ears. For a simpler version, you could use small twigs.

3 Decorate cupcakes.

Rudolph

FACE While the brown cover icing is soft, use a frilling tool to mark slightly elongated eye sockets towards the top of the face, indent the mouth with a 1 cm (½ in) vertical line at the bottom of the face and mark small dots at each side, for whisker freckles. Roll a small ball of red icing for the nose and stick it above the mouth with a dab of water. Roll small black pellets of icing for eyes, stick them in the sockets with a dab of water and paint with piping gel.

EARS Roll out brown icing to 3 mm (⅛ in) thick and cut out two ears. Roll out a thin piece of light brown icing, cut two smaller ovals for the ear interior and attach to centre of outer ears with a dab of water. Round the ears a little with your finger and insert a piece of spaghetti into the bottom edge, leaving a 2.5 cm (1 in) length extending to insert into the cupcake. Dab some water onto the cupcake where you want to place the ear and insert the spaghetti into the cake.

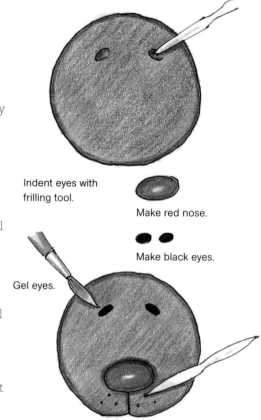

Indent eyes with frilling tool.

Make red nose.

Make black eyes.

Gel eyes.

Mark whisker dots and place nose above Rudolph's mouth.

Cut out ear shape.

Add lighter colour with a dab of water.

Insert wire or spaghetti.

FINISHING Highlight each eye with a white-white dot and rub the cheeks with a little petal dust for a rosy glow.

Paint eye highlight.

Add blush to cheeks.

Indent eyes and mouth with frilling tool.

Roll black balls and stick in eye sockets.

Make pink nose shape and indent nostrils, then attach.

Santa

FACE While the skin-coloured cover icing is still soft, mark two eye sockets and the mouth indent with a frilling tool. For the nose, roll a small ball of pink icing, indent the nostrils with a frilling tool, and stick it just below the centre of the face with a dab of water. Roll tiny black balls for the eyes and stick them into the eye sockets with a dab of water.

HAT Roll out red icing to 3 mm (1/8 in) thick and cut out a circle, using a cutter one size larger than the face. Cut off one-third, using the same cutter, and place this piece on the cupcake with a dab of water. Cut and stick a thin strip of rolled white icing along the lower edge of the hat for the trim.

Cut a large triangle of rolled red icing and fix at the top of the head with a dab of water, so that the flap falls to the front, as shown, and carefully smooth the join. Roll a large pea-sized ball of white icing for a pompom and attach to the hat with a dab of water.

Use larger cutter to make hat.

Cut out triangle section of hat.

Apply white strip and trim excess.

Roll, halve and shape a tapered sausage of icing for the moustache. Roll out a thin sausage of icing and cut out eyebrows.

EYEBROWS Roll out a thin sausage of white icing, cut two flattened lozenge shapes and stick them in place.

Petal dust

Apply blush to Santa's cheeks and mouth.

MOUSTACHE Roll a small ball of white icing into a tapered sausage, cut the sausage in half, mould each half into a moustache shape, flatten a little, then place under nose with a dab of water.

CHEEKS Mix red and pink petal dust to the desired colour and rub into the cheeks with a dry brush, to give a rosy glow.

Glaze eyes with piping gel, then add white highlights.

EARS Roll a ball of skin-coloured icing, press the frilling tool into the ball to give it an ear shape and stick it on the side of the head with a dab of water, just below the hat.

Cut out beard and apply.

Roll out a small ball for ear. Indent inner ear section and apply to Santa's head.

BEARD Using a round cutter one size larger than the cupcake, cut a disc of white icing 3 mm (1/8 in) thick, then cut a beard shape, using the diagram as a guide. Mark the beard with the back of a small knife to give it 'hair' texture and stick it on the cupcake with a dab of water.

FINISHING Paint the eyes with piping gel and allow to dry. Highlight the eyes with two tiny dots of white-white colour paste.

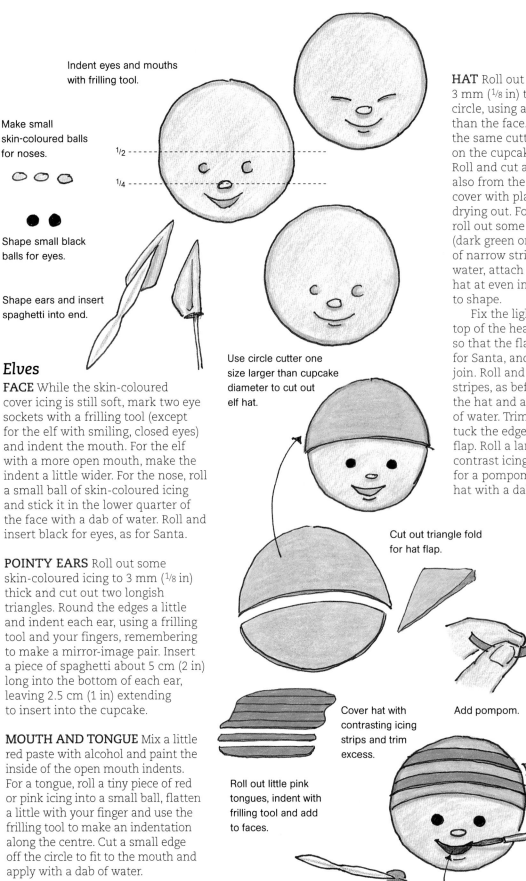

Indent eyes and mouths
with frilling tool.

Make small
skin-coloured balls
for noses.

½ - - - - - - -

¼ - - - - - - -

Shape small black
balls for eyes.

Shape ears and insert
spaghetti into end.

Elves

FACE While the skin-coloured
cover icing is still soft, mark two eye
sockets with a frilling tool (except
for the elf with smiling, closed eyes)
and indent the mouth. For the elf
with a more open mouth, make the
indent a little wider. For the nose, roll
a small ball of skin-coloured icing
and stick it in the lower quarter of
the face with a dab of water. Roll and
insert black for eyes, as for Santa.

POINTY EARS Roll out some
skin-coloured icing to 3 mm (⅛ in)
thick and cut out two longish
triangles. Round the edges a little
and indent each ear, using a frilling
tool and your fingers, remembering
to make a mirror-image pair. Insert
a piece of spaghetti about 5 cm (2 in)
long into the bottom of each ear,
leaving 2.5 cm (1 in) extending
to insert into the cupcake.

MOUTH AND TONGUE Mix a little
red paste with alcohol and paint the
inside of the open mouth indents.
For a tongue, roll a tiny piece of red
or pink icing into a small ball, flatten
a little with your finger and use the
frilling tool to make an indentation
along the centre. Cut a small edge
off the circle to fit to the mouth and
apply with a dab of water.

Use circle cutter one
size larger than cupcake
diameter to cut out
elf hat.

Cut out triangle fold
for hat flap.

Cover hat with
contrasting icing
strips and trim
excess.

Roll out little pink
tongues, indent with
frilling tool and add
to faces.

Add pompom.

Add triangle section
of hat and stripes.

Paint dark red
inside mouth.

HAT Roll out light green icing to
3 mm (⅛ in) thick and cut out a
circle, using a cutter one size larger
than the face. Cut off one-third, using
the same cutter, and place this piece
on the cupcake using a dab of water.
Roll and cut a large triangle shape,
also from the light green icing, and
cover with plastic wrap to prevent it
drying out. For the stripes on the hat,
roll out some contrast-coloured icing
(dark green or red) and cut a series
of narrow strips. Using a dab of
water, attach these strips across the
hat at even intervals and trim them
to shape.

Fix the light green triangle at the
top of the head with a dab of water,
so that the flap falls to the front, as
for Santa, and carefully smooth the
join. Roll and cut some contrast
stripes, as before, for this section of
the hat and attach them with a dab
of water. Trim the ends and gently
tuck the edges round beneath the
flap. Roll a large pea-sized ball of
contrast icing (dark green or red)
for a pompom and attach to the
hat with a dab of water.

Paint eyebrows and smiling eyes, then add blush to cheeks.

FACIAL FEATURES Mix black colour paste with some alcohol and use a fine paintbrush to paint the eyebrows and smiling eyes. Mix red and pink petal dust to the desired colour and rub into the cheeks with a dry paintbrush to give a rosy glow. For freckles, mix brown colour paste with alcohol and dot around the nose with a fine paintbrush. Paint the eyes with piping gel and allow to dry.

HAIR Using a round cutter, cut a disc of yellow (or light brown) icing, then trim to a hair shape. Make lines with a frilling tool to give texture. Mix an appropriate colour paste with alcohol and apply a little colour to the hair to make it more natural looking, if desired. Stick hair on cupcake with a dab of water.

Cut, shape and colour hair, then apply with a dab of water.

Paint on eyebrows and eyes (where applicable).

Insert ears and add eye highlights.

FINISHING Dab some water onto the cupcake where you want to place the ears and insert the extending end of spaghetti into the cake. Rub a little petal dust onto the edges of the ears, if desired. Add white-white colour paste highlight dots to each eye.

Bad-mannered monsters

The idea behind these cheeky characters is that you create whatever horrible monsters you wish. I'm sure the kids will be able to help you with this! You can copy our designs, or mix and match the features of several different monsters to create your own.

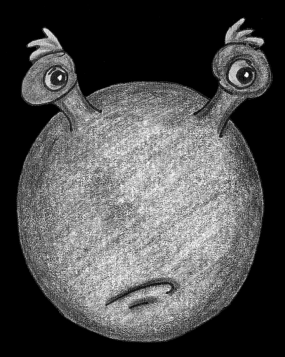

Materials

12 ganached cupcakes
125 ml (4 fl oz/½ cup) syrup
Cornflour in shaker
1.2 kg (2 lb 10 oz) fondant icing
Colour paste: red, yellow, brown,
    black, green, purple, pink,
    teal, white-white
Red and pink petal dust
Cake-decorating alcohol
Airbrush colours of your choice
Piping gel
Dried spaghetti
Tylose powder

Equipment

Large and small rolling pins
Cranked palette knife
Small sharp kitchen knife
Flexi-smoother
Pastry brush
Frilling tool
Balling tool
Fine and medium paintbrushes
Airbrush machine
Circle cutters
50 cm (20 in) square cake board
    (optional)

Techniques checklist

Recipes (page 204)
Ganaching cupcakes (page 208)
Colouring fondant icing
    (page 210)
Red and black icing (page 211)
Skin-coloured icing (page 211)
Covering cupcakes (page 209)
Eyes (page 215)
Blush (page 214)
Gelling (page 213)
Airbrushing (page 216)

Step-by-step

1 Colour fondant icing. Mix colours the day before if possible, to make intense colours easier to work with. You will require about 40 g (1½ oz) icing for the cover of each cupcake, as well as small amounts of a variety of colours for the decoration.

2 Cover cupcakes. It is best to cover and complete each different type of cake individually, rather than covering them all at once. Allow about 40 g (1½ oz) icing per cupcake and roll the icing out to 3 mm (⅛ in) thick. Cover the ganached cupcakes in colours of your choice (or to match our monsters), using orange, yellow, brown, green, white, purple, hot pink, teal and skin-colour.

3 Decorate cupcakes.

Furry monster

FACE Roll icing to 6 mm (¼ in) thick, instead of 3 mm (⅛ in), and cut cover with a circle cutter one size larger than the top of the cupcake. Before placing it on the cake, use a small sharp knife to cut out an open mouth shape. You can also use the knife to cut around the edge of the icing in a jagged fashion to create the illusion of fur. Set the cut-out mouth aside and cover the cupcake with the disc. Roll out a very thin layer of contrast-colour icing (such as black or red) and use the cut-out mouth shape as a template to cut a similar-shaped piece. Insert the contrast shape into the mouth hole on the cake and smooth in place.

EYES, NOSE AND TEETH For eyes, roll two balls of yellow or light brown icing and adhere them to the eye sockets with a dab of water. Mix black colour paste with alcohol and paint the pupils. For the nose, roll a coloured ball, indent the nostrils with a frilling tool and adhere to the face. Roll out a thin sausage of white icing and cut several small, lozenge-shaped teeth. Adhere them to the mouth with a dab of water. Roll out a thin layer of red icing and cut a tongue shape. Add the centre indent with a frilling tool and adhere to the mouth. Paint eyes, teeth and tongue with piping gel, allow to dry, then add white-white colour paste highlights to the eyes.

Cut out an open mouth shape.

Indent eye sockets with a balling tool.

Mark fur with a frilling tool.

Use cut-out mouth as template for contrast mouth.

Indent nostrils with a frilling tool and adhere nose to face.

FUR Mark the monster's fur using the frilling tool and use the balling tool to indent two eye sockets. Airbrush the cupcake to highlight the fur, using a semi-circular thin cardboard mask to protect the sides of the cake from the spray (see page 98).

Protect cupcake with cardboard mask while airbrushing.

Adhere teeth, tongue and eyes to face, then paint eyes with piping gel and add highlights.

Monster with antenna eyes

FACE Roll out icing to 3 mm ($\frac{1}{8}$ in) thick and cut out a cover one size larger than the top of the cupcake. Cut out a mouth shape (as for Furry monster, opposite) before covering cake. Use the cut-out mouth as a template to cut a contrast mouth from thinly rolled icing. Insert this piece into the mouth and smooth in place. For the gums, cut another mouth shape from thinly rolled pink icing and cut it in half, removing a strip from the middle. Use a frilling tool to make indents in each piece for the teeth. Stick the gums into the mouth with a dab of water. Roll out a thin sausage of white icing, cut lozenge-shaped teeth and attach them to the gums with a dab of water. Roll and shape a nose with a frilling tool and adhere to the face. For the lips, roll a thin sausage of contrast icing and glue it around the mouth with a dab of water, cutting and smoothing the ends to make a seamless join.

For the gums, cut out a mouth shape, then cut in half and cut a strip from the middle.

Use a frilling tool to make tooth indents in the gums.

ANTENNA EYES For the eyes, insert two lengths of spaghetti into the top of the cupcake, leaving about 3 cm ($1\frac{1}{4}$ in) extending. Roll and cut a strip of icing to wrap around each extending end. Adhere these strips around the spaghetti, smoothing them in place and trimming to leave a small amount of spaghetti still extending to skewer the balls for the eye sockets. Roll two small balls of icing for the eye sockets and push each one gently onto the extending spaghetti. Use a balling tool to indent eye sockets. Roll two tiny black balls for the eyes and glue them into the eye sockets with water. Paint them with piping gel and, when dry, add white-white colour paste highlights.

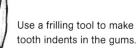

Insert two lengths of spaghetti into head with 3 cm ($1\frac{1}{4}$ in) extending.

Cut strips of icing to wrap around extending spaghetti for antennae.

Indent nostrils into nose and adhere to face with water.

Roll a thin sausage of icing for lips and glue around mouth.

Use a balling tool to indent eye sockets.

For eye sockets, roll two balls of icing and push each gently into extending spaghetti.

Roll two tiny black balls of icing for eyes and add to sockets. Paint with piping gel, then add highlights.

HAIR, HORNS AND HATS All of these appendages are added to the monsters in the same way and can be in any shape you like. Remember to insert a supporting skewer of spaghetti into each one, or mould the shapes themselves around the spaghetti, leaving enough spaghetti extending to insert into the cake. Always use a dab of water to stick one piece of icing to another, even when you're using a skewer. To make a hat, roll and cut a small circle for the brim, then roll a small ball and shape it with a frilling tool, as shown. Adhere the top to the brim and add a thin hatband.

Make any appendage you like and shape it around spaghetti.

Roll a small circle for a hat brim, an indented semi-circle for the top and a thin hatband.

INDENTED MOUTHS While the cover icing is still soft, use the edge of a round cutter or frilling tool to indent the mouth and make a smile or grimace. To make a surprised mouth, insert the frilling tool into the cover and lift it up a little, pulling the shape into an 'O'. Leave these mouths just as they are, or use black or red paste mixed with alcohol to highlight the indent. Wherever you plan to add teeth, press slight indents into the area where you want to place them — it makes them look much more natural.

Indent mouth with a frilling tool. Make slight indents for teeth before adding.

For a surprised mouth, insert frilling tool into cover, lift and pull it into an 'O' shape.

Shape and attach ears to cupcake.

Cut jagged teeth from a strip of white icing mixed with Tylose powder. Allow to dry before adding to face.

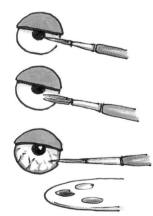

BLOODSHOT EYES While the cover icing is still soft, use a balling tool to make two indents for the eye sockets. Roll two small pea-sized balls of white icing. From a thinly rolled contrast colour, cut a small circle and divide in half into two crescent-shaped eyelids. Glue the eyelids in place on the eyeballs with a little water. Using black paste mixed with alcohol, paint the eyeline and the pupil and allow to dry. Paint the exposed eyeball with piping gel and allow to dry. Using red paste mixed with alcohol, paint in the red blood vessels with a fine paintbrush. Add white-white colour paste highlights and glue the finished eyes into the sockets with a little water.

Paint eyeball with piping gel, then paint in the red blood vessels.

EARS AND JAGGED TEETH Ears are added in the same way as hair, horns and hats. Roll and cut a basic ear shape, then adhere a thinner, smaller inner ear to the outer ear and insert a spaghetti skewer into the bottom, leaving enough extending to insert into the cupcake. Once you have made each ear, you can gently mould them with your fingers into a more realistic, rounded shape. Dab some water onto the cupcake where you want to place the ear and insert the extending end of the spaghetti into the cake. To make jagged teeth, add a little Tylose powder to a ball of white icing (to make it dry harder) and roll it out to 3 mm ($1/8$ in) thick. Cut a 1.5 cm-wide ($5/8$ in) strip with a clean knife, cut into zigzag shapes for the teeth and leave to dry. Stick the hardened teeth around the rim of the cupcake with a dab of water.

Naughty boys

FACES To make a face with puffed cheeks, cover a cupcake with a thinly rolled disc of skin-coloured icing. Roll two large pea-sized balls of icing, flatten slightly and adhere to the cover with a dab of water. Now roll and cut another disc of skin-coloured icing and gently stretch it over the original cover, smoothing it carefully. Make mouth and eye socket indents, as shown, rolling and adding skin-coloured balls for the nose and ears, and small white balls for the eyes. Flatten a small red ball into a tongue shape and indent with the frilling tool. Adhere it to the mouth indent with a dab of water.

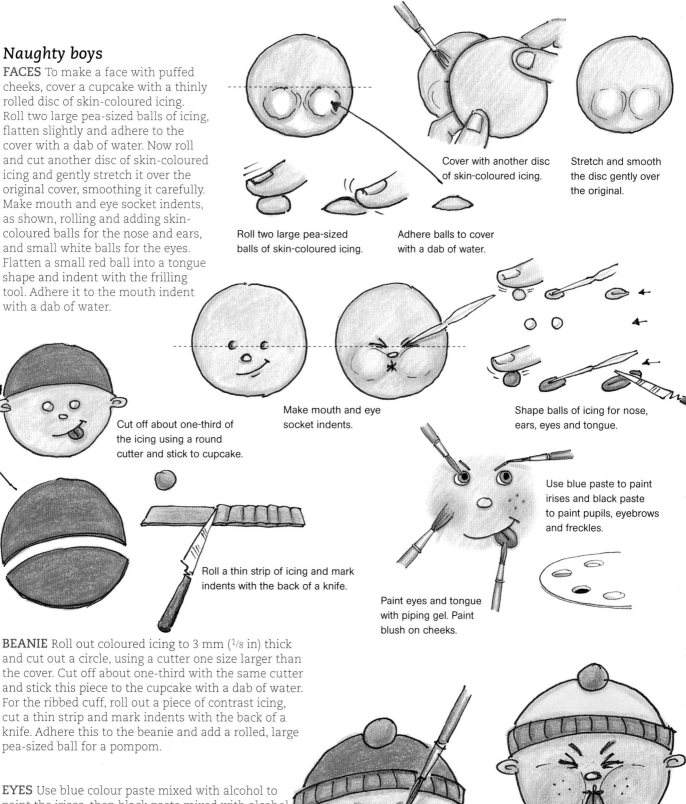

Cover with another disc of skin-coloured icing.

Stretch and smooth the disc gently over the original.

Roll two large pea-sized balls of skin-coloured icing.

Adhere balls to cover with a dab of water.

Make mouth and eye socket indents.

Shape balls of icing for nose, ears, eyes and tongue.

Cut off about one-third of the icing using a round cutter and stick to cupcake.

Roll a thin strip of icing and mark indents with the back of a knife.

Use blue paste to paint irises and black paste to paint pupils, eyebrows and freckles.

Paint eyes and tongue with piping gel. Paint blush on cheeks.

BEANIE Roll out coloured icing to 3 mm (1/8 in) thick and cut out a circle, using a cutter one size larger than the cover. Cut off about one-third with the same cutter and stick this piece to the cupcake with a dab of water. For the ribbed cuff, roll out a piece of contrast icing, cut a thin strip and mark indents with the back of a knife. Adhere this to the beanie and add a rolled, large pea-sized ball for a pompom.

EYES Use blue colour paste mixed with alcohol to paint the irises, then black paste mixed with alcohol to paint the pupils, eyebrows and freckles. For the closed eyes, paint two lines like chopsticks meeting, as shown. Paint eyes and tongue with piping gel, rub petal dust into the cheeks with a dry paintbrush and finish eyes with white-white colour paste highlights.

Finish eyes with highlights.

Mosaics

A mosaic is one of the most effective ways of presenting a collection of cupcakes — each one different, each one a part of the whole design, just like the tiles in a 'real' mosaic. Choose one of our mosaic templates or adapt the technique to your own special design.

Pulsating heart

This design is a great introduction to making a mosaic from a related series of cupcakes. Rainbow colours also look amazing for these cakes. It's a very special way to tell someone you love them.

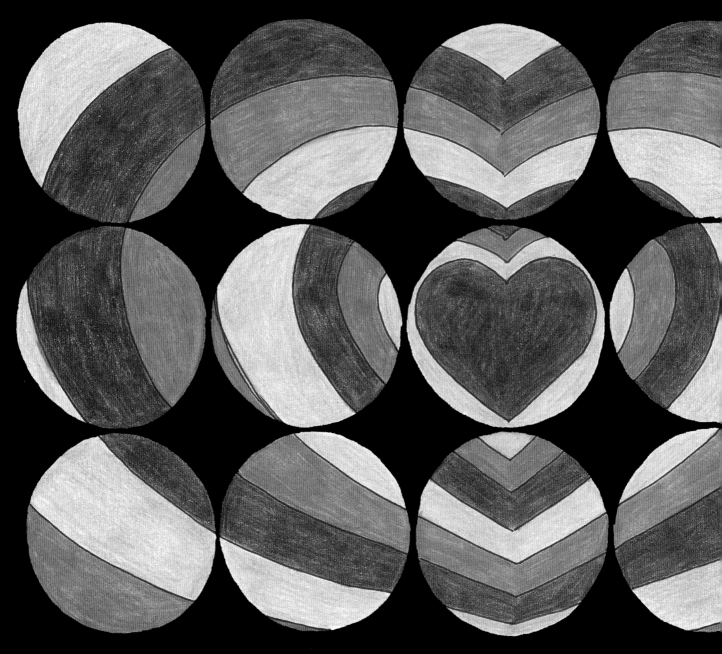

Materials

15 cupcakes, tops trimmed flat
    and ganached
160 ml (5¼ fl oz) syrup
Cornflour in shaker
1.4 kg (3 lb 2 oz) fondant icing
Colour paste: red, pink

Equipment

2B pencil and tracing paper
Large and small rolling pins
Cranked palette knife
Small sharp kitchen knife
Flexi-smoother
Pastry brush
Fine and medium paintbrushes
Circle cutters
Bamboo skewer (optional)
6 cm (2½ in) heart cutter
    (optional)
50 cm (20 in) square cake
    board (optional)

Techniques checklist

Step-by-step

1 Make mosaic template. Follow the steps on page 222 to trace and transfer the pulsating heart template on pages 224 and 225.

2 Colour fondant icing. Mix the colours the day before, so the intense colours are easier to work with, particularly the red. You will need about 600 g (1 lb 5 oz) of light pink and 400 g (14 oz) each of red and hot pink.

3 Cut covers. Cut and decorate all the mosaic covers completely before adhering them to the cupcakes. This allows you to manipulate the design more easily on a flat surface. Roll out light pink icing to a rectangle about 30 cm x 45 cm x 3 mm thick (12 x 18 x 1/8 in) — this should be large enough to cover fifteen 7 cm (2¾ in) cupcakes. Cover the rolled icing with vinyl or a double thickness of plastic wrap to prevent drying, and cut and remove one disc at a time. Smooth the edge of the disc with your fingers, check it against the cutter again and trim if necessary. Cut fifteen discs in this way.

Roll out light pink icing to 3 mm (1/8 in) thick.

Cover to prevent drying.

Cut and remove one disc at a time and smooth edge.

Check size with the circle cutter.

Cut centre heart and adhere to disc.

Place 15 discs in a 5 x 3 grid and lay template over discs. Transfer template by rubbing with your hand or a bamboo skewer.

Lift one corner to check that transfer is working.

4 Transfer template. Arrange the discs in their final grid pattern, lay the template on top, pencil-side down, and move the discs until they align with the template. Hold the template in place with a few pieces of tape and rub over it with your hand or a skewer to transfer the design to the icing.

5 Decorate cupcakes.

RED HEART CENTRE Roll out a walnut-sized ball of red icing to about 3 mm (1/8 in) thick or a little thinner. Using the heart cutter or the heart template and a knife, cut out the centre heart, smooth the edges with your fingers and adhere it to the top of the centre cover disc with a dab of water.

HOT PINK PULSATING LINES

Roll out hot-pink icing to about the same dimensions as the light pink icing, but rolling it slightly thinner. Cover with the template and rub over with your hand or a skewer to transfer the design. Using the photograph as a guide, cut out the hot-pink heart shapes of the design with a small sharp knife. Remove any excess icing, leaving the marked areas that you need to use. Cover icing with a double thickness of plastic wrap to prevent drying.

Use circle cutters to remove the required segments, smooth the edges with your fingers and attach the segments to the corresponding cover discs with a dab of water.

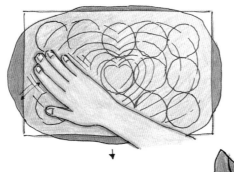

Roll out hot-pink icing, cover with template and transfer pattern.

Cut around shapes and remove unnecessary icing.

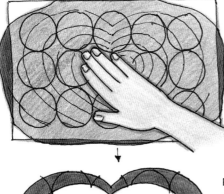

Icing can be manipulated into place while still soft.

Use circle cutters to remove required segments.

RED PULSATING LINES Roll out the red icing as before and, using the template again, transfer the design to the icing. Cut out, smooth and adhere the segments to the relevant cover with a dab of water. Any remaining pencil lines can be gently removed with a damp brush.

Repeat process with red icing.

6 Cover cupcakes. Apply syrup to the top of the levelled and ganached cupcakes and adhere the covers in place. Smooth and polish the icing with a flexi-smoother to make sure the joins are perfectly smooth and flush. Arrange in their mosaic order.

Brush syrup on levelled and ganached cupcakes, and attach covers.

Go dog, go!

This is a fine example of how cupcakes can work as a mosaic. The roads link all the cupcakes together, but the dogs and other components remain intact in their own little scenes. These cupcakes are an instant hit with all ages, so let your imagination go wild and see if you can improve on our design.

Materials

15 cupcakes, tops trimmed flat
    and ganached
160 ml (5¼ fl oz) syrup
Cornflour in shaker
1.4 kg (3 lb 2 oz) fondant icing
Colour paste: green, red,
    pink, yellow, black, orange,
    purple, brown
Cake-decorating alcohol
Royal icing

Equipment

2B pencil and tracing paper
Large and small rolling pins
Cranked palette knife
Small sharp kitchen knife
Flexi-smoother
Pastry brush
Fine and medium paintbrushes
Circle cutters
Small flower cutter (optional)
Bamboo skewers
50 cm (20 in) square cake board
    (optional)
Paint palette
Piping bag
No. 1 and No. 2 piping tips

Techniques checklist

Recipes (page 204)
Ganaching cupcakes (page 208)
Making a template (page 221)
Colouring fondant icing
    (page 210)
Covering cupcakes (page 209)
Transferring a template
    (page 221)
Templates for mosaics
    (page 222)
Red and black icing (page 211)
Piping with royal icing
    (page 217)
Edible painting and colour wash
    (page 213)

Step-by-step

1 Make mosaic template. Follow the steps on page 222 to trace and transfer the Go dog, go! template on pages 226 and 227.

2 Colour fondant icing. Mix the colours the day before if possible, so the intense colours are easier to work with. You will need small amounts of green, light blue, red, white, hot pink, yellow, black, orange, purple, light beige and brown, plus 600 g (1 lb 5 oz) bright green (use green and a little yellow colour paste) for the covers.

3 Cut covers. Cut and decorate all the mosaic covers completely before adhering them to the cupcakes. This allows you to manipulate the design more easily on a flat surface. Roll out bright green icing to a rectangle about 30 cm x 45 cm x 3 mm thick (12 x 18 x $^1/_8$ in) — this should be large enough to cover fifteen 7 cm (2$^3/_4$ in) cupcakes. Cover the rolled icing with vinyl or a double thickness of plastic wrap to prevent drying, and cut and remove one disc at a time. Smooth the edge of the disc with your fingers, check it against the cutter again and trim if necessary. Cut 15 discs in this way.

4 Transfer template. Arrange the discs in their final grid pattern, lay the template on top, pencil-side down, and move the discs until they align with the template. Hold the template in place with a few pieces of tape and rub over it with your hand or a skewer to transfer the design to the icing.

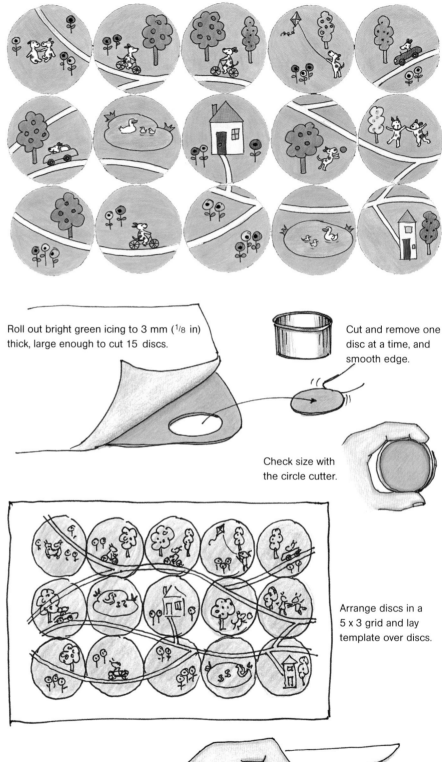

Roll out bright green icing to 3 mm ($^1/_8$ in) thick, large enough to cut 15 discs.

Cut and remove one disc at a time, and smooth edge.

Check size with the circle cutter.

Arrange discs in a 5 x 3 grid and lay template over discs.

Transfer template by rubbing with your hand or a bamboo skewer.

Lift one corner to check that transfer is working.

5 Decorate cupcakes.

ROADS Roll out light beige icing to about the same dimensions as the bright green icing, but rolling it slightly thinner. Cover with the template and rub over it with your hand or a bamboo skewer to transfer the design. Cut along the lines of the road and remove any excess icing, leaving the marked areas you need to use. Cover icing with plastic wrap to prevent drying. (Leftover beige icing can be used as a base colour for darker yellow, orange and brown.)

Use circle cutters to remove the required segments of road. Smooth the edges with your fingers and apply each segment to the corresponding cover disc with a dab of water.

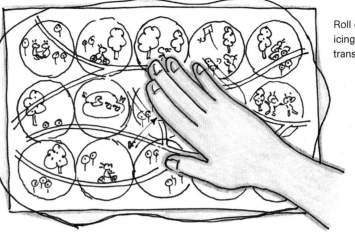

Roll out light beige icing for the road and transfer the template.

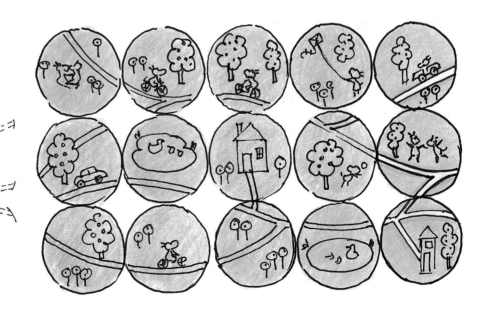

Cut along lines of road and remove unnecessary icing.

Use circle cutter to remove required segments, smooth edges and apply to corresponding discs.

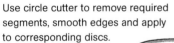

Cover to prevent drying out.

TREES Thinly roll out green and various other colours of your choice and, using the templates and a small sharp knife, cut out tree shapes, as pictured. Alternatively, use a five-petal flower cutter, then stretch the shape gently with your fingers so that it is less regular. For the tree trunks, roll out brown icing and cut strips to match size of trees. Place the trees and trunks in position and stick with a dab of water. For the fruit on the trees, take walnut-sized balls of red or orange icing, pinch off tiny pieces, roll them into balls, squash them flat and place them on the trees with a dab of water. If you prefer, you can also mix some red and/or black royal icing and pipe red or black dots onto the tree using a No. 2 piping tip.

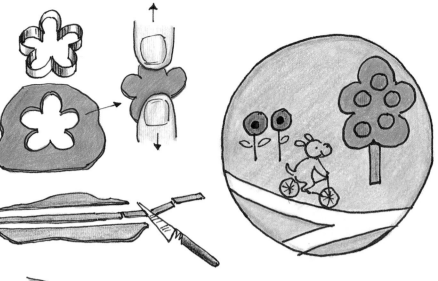

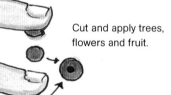

Cut and apply trees, flowers and fruit.

FLOWERS Roll grape-sized balls of various colours, as well as black. Pinch off small balls of coloured icing, squash them flat and attach to the covers with a dab of water wherever you would like them. Pinch off tiny balls of black icing, squash them flat and place them in the centre of each 'flower' with a dab of water.

Cut and apply dog shapes.

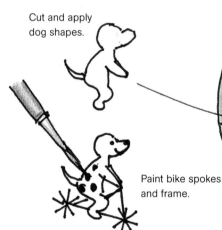

Paint bike spokes and frame.

Paint eyes, mouth, nose and spots.

Pipe dogs' ears and bike wheels.

DOGS, CARS AND BIKES Roll out white, red and blue icing to 3 mm (1/8 in) thick and, using the templates, cut out dogs and cars from the appropriate colour with a sharp knife.

Apply to the relevant icing cover disc with a dab of water. Add details to the cars, as shown. Mix black colour paste with alcohol and paint eyes, mouth, nose, spots, bicycle frames and wheel spokes. Mix up black royal icing and, using a No. 1 piping tip, pipe on the dogs' ears and the bicycle wheels.

PONDS AND DUCKS Roll out a walnut-sized ball of light blue icing to 3 mm (¹/₈ in) thick. Use the template or work freehand to cut the pond shapes and adhere them to the covers, as shown, with a dab of water. Cut duck and duckling shapes from white and yellow icing and adhere to ponds.

HOUSES Thinly roll out icing in the desired colours for the houses. Using a small sharp knife, cut out the components for the two houses, either freehand or using the template. Cut windows, doors, roofs, chimneys and roll tiny balls of icing for the doorknobs. Assemble all the pieces on the relevant icing covers.

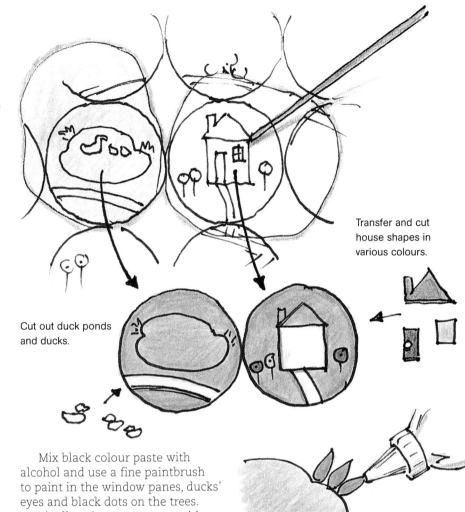

Transfer and cut house shapes in various colours.

Cut out duck ponds and ducks.

FINISHING Using a No. 1 piping tip and green royal icing, pipe flower stems, leaves and grass, as shown.

Roll out thin scraps of coloured icing and cut and assemble the kite on the relevant icing cover. Using a No. 1 piping tip and black royal icing, pipe the kite string and tail. Roll and cut tiny coloured tail ribbons and attach to the tail after it is piped.

Mix black colour paste with alcohol and use a fine paintbrush to paint in the window panes, ducks' eyes and black dots on the trees.

Finally, mix orange paste with alcohol and paint in the beaks on the ducks and ducklings. Arrange the cupcakes in their mosaic order.

Pipe stems, leaves and grass.

Pipe stems, leaves and grass.

Paint details on ducks, windows and trees.

Make and assemble kite, then pipe kite string and attach ribbons to tail.

Mix-n-match Betty Sue

This mix-n-match story was inspired by a children's book I had when I was growing up. I especially loved matching the pretty ladies with hairy men's legs. The robot was inspired by a design from my friend, Naomi, of Hello Naomi in Newcastle, Australia.

Materials

15 cupcakes, tops trimmed flat and ganached
160 ml (5¼ fl oz) syrup
Cornflour in shaker
1.4 kg (3 lb 2 oz) fondant icing
Colour paste: green, yellow, black, red, blue, brown, pink, orange, white-white
Cake-decorating alcohol
Royal icing
Edible gold and silver dust
Red and pink petal dust
Edible glitter: purple
Piping gel

Equipment

2B pencil and tracing paper
Large and small rolling pins
Cranked palette knife
Small sharp kitchen knife
Flexi-smoother
Pastry brush
Frilling tool
Fine and medium paintbrushes
Paint palette
Round cutters
Small flower cutters
No. 4 and No. 8 piping tips
    (optional)
50 cm (20 in) square cake board
    (optional)

Techniques checklist

Step-by-step

1 Make mosaic template. Follow the steps on page 222 to trace and transfer the Mix-n-match Betty Sue template on pages 228 and 229.

2 Colour fondant icing. Mix the colours the day before if possible, so the intense colours are easier to work with. You need to mix small amounts of khaki, skin-colour, yellow, black, red, blue, brown, hot pink and burnt orange. You also need 600 g (1 lb 5 oz) of white for the covers.

3 Cut covers. Cut and decorate all the mosaic covers completely before adhering them to the cupcakes. This allows you to manipulate the design more easily on a flat surface.

Roll out white icing to a rectangle about 30 cm x 45 cm x 3 mm thick (12 x 18 x 1/8 in) — this should be large enough to cover fifteen 7 cm (2 3/4 in) cupcakes. Cover the rolled icing with vinyl or a double thickness of plastic wrap to prevent drying, and cut and remove one disc at a time. Smooth the edge of the disc with your fingers, check it against the cutter again and trim if necessary. Cut 15 discs in this way.

4 Transfer template. Arrange the discs in their final grid pattern, lay the template on top, pencil-side down, and move the discs until they align with the template. Hold the template in place with a few pieces of tape and rub over it with your hand or a skewer to transfer the design to the icing.

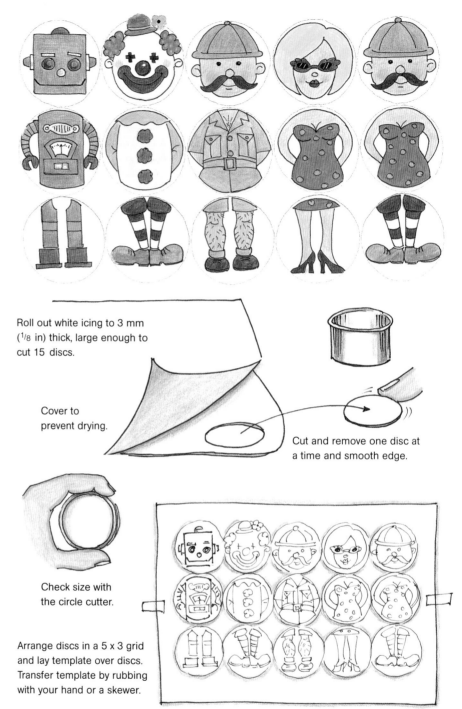

Roll out white icing to 3 mm (1/8 in) thick, large enough to cut 15 discs.

Cover to prevent drying.

Cut and remove one disc at a time and smooth edge.

Check size with the circle cutter.

Arrange discs in a 5 x 3 grid and lay template over discs. Transfer template by rubbing with your hand or a skewer.

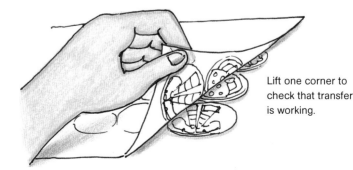

Lift one corner to check that transfer is working.

5 Decorate cupcakes.

Betty Sue

BODY Roll out skin-coloured icing to 3 mm (⅛ in) thick. Lay the template, pencil-side down, on top and transfer the Betty Sue details to the icing. Cut out the skin-coloured sections of the design and attach to the relevant cover discs with a dab of water.

Roll out skin-coloured icing and transfer Betty Sue's skin details.

Cut out skin-coloured details and transfer to cover discs.

HAIR Roll out yellow icing, transfer the hair outline from the template, cut out and adhere to the disc.

FACE Roll a tiny round pink nose and heart-shaped red lips and attach to the face. Indent the mouth with a frilling tool.

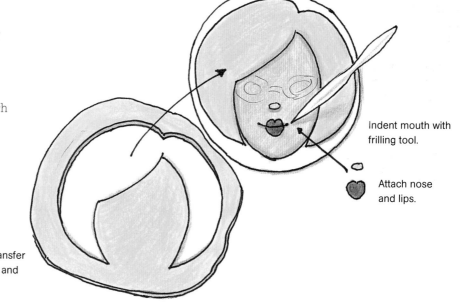

Indent mouth with frilling tool.

Attach nose and lips.

Roll out icing for hair, transfer image, then cut out hair and transfer to cover disc.

DRESS Roll out hot-pink icing and use the template to trace Betty Sue's dress. Cut out and adhere to the cover discs. Use a frilling tool to mark Betty Sue's décolletage.

Make yellow spots for the dress by cutting them with the end of a No. 8 piping tip or by rolling and squashing tiny balls. Glue to the dress with a dab of water.

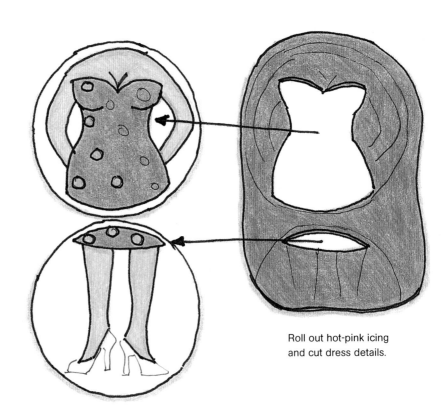

Make and apply spots for dress.

Roll out hot-pink icing and cut dress details.

SHOES AND GLASSES Trace and cut shoes and sunglasses from thin purple icing. Paint with piping gel, leaving the lens area of the glasses gel-free. Sprinkle with edible glitter and press gently to help it stick.

Allow to dry, then brush away excess glitter with a soft brush. Attach finished pieces to the appropriate disc. Mix black colour paste with alcohol and paint the glasses' lenses.

Trace and cut sunglasses and shoes.

Paint with gel and apply glitter.

Sprinkle with glitter, then brush away excess.

Attach sunglasses and shoes to discs and paint glasses' lenses black.

Explorer, clown and robot

Work on one character at a time, and keep the discs well covered with vinyl or plastic wrap when not in use.

COSTUMES Working in the same way as for Betty Sue, roll out the skin and costume colours, one colour at a time. Transfer the design, cut out the relevant pieces and adhere them to the appropriate cover discs. Use small flower cutters to cut the clown's hair and hat flower.

INDENTED DETAILS While the icing is still soft, use a frilling tool or the back of a small knife to indent the face and costume markings, such as mouths, ears, eye sockets, elbows, knees, the pockets on the safari suit and hat, shoes, the ribbed sleeves of the robot's suit, and so on. Use a No. 4 piping tip to indent the buttons on the safari suit.

NOSES AND EYES Roll small balls of the appropriate colour and adhere them to the face with a dab of water. Roll tiny black balls and attach them to the eye sockets on the explorer and clown.

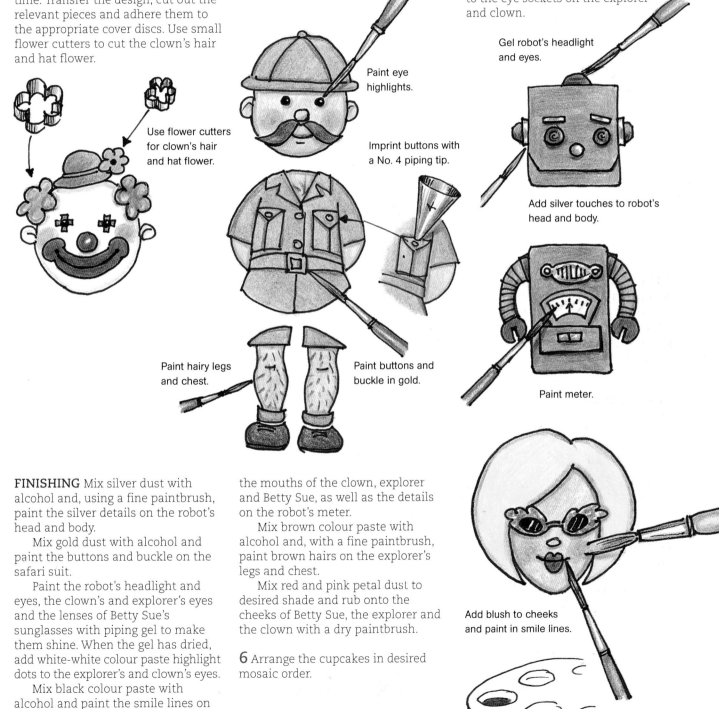

Use flower cutters for clown's hair and hat flower.

Paint eye highlights.

Imprint buttons with a No. 4 piping tip.

Gel robot's headlight and eyes.

Add silver touches to robot's head and body.

Paint hairy legs and chest.

Paint buttons and buckle in gold.

Paint meter.

Add blush to cheeks and paint in smile lines.

FINISHING Mix silver dust with alcohol and, using a fine paintbrush, paint the silver details on the robot's head and body.

Mix gold dust with alcohol and paint the buttons and buckle on the safari suit.

Paint the robot's headlight and eyes, the clown's and explorer's eyes and the lenses of Betty Sue's sunglasses with piping gel to make them shine. When the gel has dried, add white-white colour paste highlight dots to the explorer's and clown's eyes.

Mix black colour paste with alcohol and paint the smile lines on the mouths of the clown, explorer and Betty Sue, as well as the details on the robot's meter.

Mix brown colour paste with alcohol and, with a fine paintbrush, paint brown hairs on the explorer's legs and chest.

Mix red and pink petal dust to desired shade and rub onto the cheeks of Betty Sue, the explorer and the clown with a dry paintbrush.

6 Arrange the cupcakes in desired mosaic order.

Rainbow dragon

Our dragon was born in a moment of fantasy and we could not resist including it. However, the idea was to inspire you creatively and show you what is possible once you start to think outside the box. This mosaic could easily be applied to crocodiles, lizards and snakes.

Materials

14 cupcakes, tops trimmed flat and ganached
160 ml (5¼ fl oz) syrup
Cornflour in shaker
1 kg (3 lb 5 oz) fondant icing
Colour paste: green, yellow, black, red, blue, brown, pink, orange, white-white
Tylose powder
Airbrush colour: brown, yellow
Cake-decorating alcohol
Piping gel
Royal icing (optional)

Equipment

2B pencil and tracing paper
Large and small rolling pins
Cranked palette knife
Small sharp kitchen knife
Fla -smoother
Pastry brush
Frilling tool
Fine and medium paintbrushes
22-gauge florist's wire
Piping bag
No. 2 piping tip
7 cm (2¾ in) and 2 cm (¾ in) circle cutters
Bamboo skewer
Airbrush machine
50 cm (20 in) square cake board (optional)

Techniques checklist

Recipes (page 204)
Ganaching cupcakes (page 208)
Making a template (page 221)
Colouring fondant icing (page 210)
Red and black icing (page 211)
Covering cupcakes (page 209)
Transferring a template (page 221)
Templates for mosaics (page 222)
Airbrushing (page 216)
Eyes (page 215)
Gelling (page 213)
Edible painting and colour wash (page 213)

Step-by-step

1 Make mosaic template. Follow the steps on page 222 to trace and transfer the Rainbow dragon template on pages 230 and 231.

2 Colour fondant icing. Mix the colours the day before if possible, so the intense colours are easier to work with. You need about 600 g (1 lb 5 oz) black icing for the covers and about 250 g (9 oz) golden ochre icing (made by using yellow and brown colour paste) for the body parts. You will also need an apple-sized ball each of green, red, pink, blue, light blue, black and yellow icing (for the scales).

3 Cut covers. Cut and decorate all the mosaic covers completely before adhering them to the cupcakes. This allows you to manipulate the design more easily on a flat surface.

Roll out black icing to a rectangle about 30 cm x 45 cm x 3 mm thick (12 x 18 x 1/8 in) — this should be large enough to cover fourteen 7 cm (2¾ in) cupcakes. Cover the rolled icing with vinyl or a double thickness of plastic wrap to prevent drying, and cut and remove one disc at a time. Smooth the edge of the disc with your fingers, check it against the cutter again and trim if necessary. Cut out 14 discs and cover them with plastic wrap until they are needed.

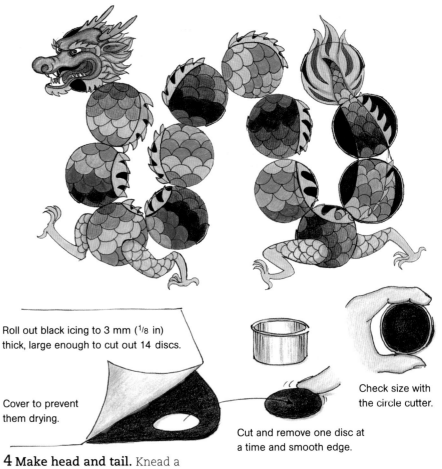

Roll out black icing to 3 mm (1/8 in) thick, large enough to cut out 14 discs.

Cover to prevent them drying.

Cut and remove one disc at a time and smooth edge.

Check size with the circle cutter.

4 Make head and tail. Knead a little Tylose powder into the golden ochre icing to harden the body pieces. Roll out the icing to 3 mm (1/8 in) thick and, using the templates, transfer the head and tail outlines onto the icing. Using a sharp knife, cut out the shapes and smooth with your fingers, making sure to keep them (and any excess icing) well covered when you are not working on them. Cut two wires, about

7.5 cm (3 in) long, and insert them into the snout and lower jaw of the head for extra support. Use a frilling tool to indent along the traced features of both head and tail, to add 3D definition. For the dragon's ear, cut a teardrop of icing, approximately 3 cm (1¼ in) long, and indent with the frilling tool. Attach the ear to the side of the dragon's head with a dab of water.

Roll out golden ochre icing mixed with Tylose and transfer head and tail details.

Indent along definition lines with a frilling tool.

Cut out ear, indent and attach to head.

Cut out head and tail.

5 Make legs. Roll out golden ochre icing and use the templates to transfer and cut the front and back legs. Use a round cutter to remove the excess sections of icing where the legs will fit against the cupcake body. Insert support wires into the legs where needed, as shown, leaving a length of wire extending for insertion into the cupcake when the dragon is assembled. Smooth the legs with your fingers and mark the scales on the upper section of each leg with a frilling tool.

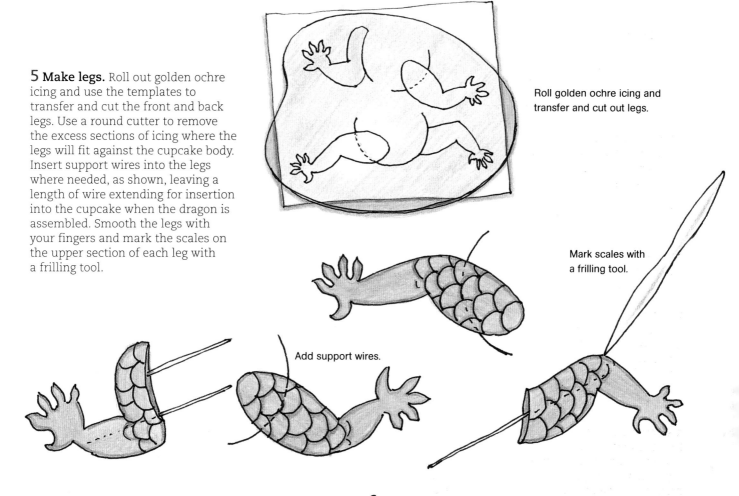

Roll golden ochre icing and transfer and cut out legs.

Mark scales with a frilling tool.

Add support wires.

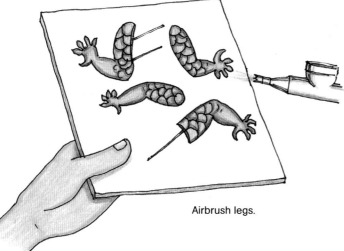

Airbrush legs.

6 Airbrush body parts. Fill the reservoir on the airbrush with alcohol and add one drop of brown airbrush colour. Carefully spray around the edges of the head and tail, then spray over the indented lines. Do the same for the legs, spraying around the edges of the legs as well as along the indented scale lines.

Clean the airbrush thoroughly, then fill the reservoir with alcohol again, and add one drop of yellow colour. Sweep-spray across the head, tail and legs, giving a nice golden effect. Allow to dry.

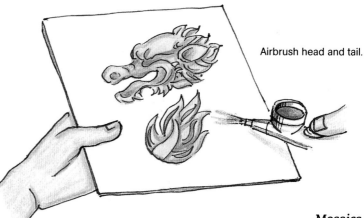

Airbrush head and tail.

7 Add dragon's face and tail details. Using the picture as a guide to colours, roll out each colour, one at a time, to about 2 mm ($^1/_{16}$ in) thick with a small rolling pin. Using the template and a sharp knife, cut out the details for the dragon's face and tail, starting with the gums, tongue and flames, then moving on to the teeth, eyes and eyebrows. Work quickly and cover the pieces as soon as possible so that they don't dry out. Glue the details on with a dab of water, taking care not to get any liquid on areas that will remain exposed.

Mix black colour paste and alcohol and paint the pupils on the eyes with a fine paintbrush. Allow to dry and paint the eye and pupil with piping gel to make it shine. When the gel is dry, add tiny white-white colour paste highlights.

Roll out colours thinly and cut out gums, tongue and flames.

Add coloured details to head and tail.

Arrange 12 discs in dragon pattern and lay template over discs.

8 Cut and add scales. Arrange 12 of the black-icing cover discs into the design for the dragon's body. Lay the template, pencil-side down, over the discs, rearranging the discs as necessary so that they align with the circle outlines on the template. Use a bamboo skewer to trace over the edges of the dragon's body, the areas where the spine twists and the start of each change of scale colour.

Roll out each of the seven colours for the scales, one at a time, with a small rolling pin and cover to prevent them from drying out. The largest scales are cut with a 2 cm (¾ in) round cutter. We use various piping tips to cut the smaller scales, but you can also roll small balls and press them flat with your finger.

Overlap the scales onto the cover discs, fixing each one with a dab of

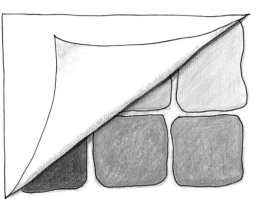

Roll out seven colours for scales.

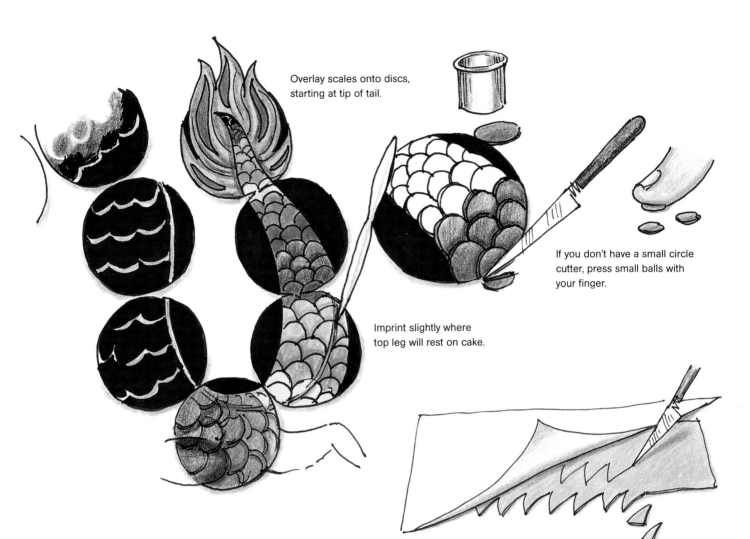

Overlay scales onto discs, starting at tip of tail.

If you don't have a small circle cutter, press small balls with your finger.

Imprint slightly where top leg will rest on cake.

Cut spines and attach to discs.

water, starting with the smallest circles at the tail and increasing in size as you move along the body.

Before decorating the very tip of the tail, attach the decorated golden-ochre tail section to a plain black cover with a dab of water. To get a good fit at the tip of the tail, place the scales out in position on the benchtop, then lay the tail template over the top and trim the outside scales to the shape of the tail with a sharp knife.

As you work, use your fingers to slightly flatten the section of each scale that will be covered by the next one. Using a sharp knife or the round cutter, trim off any excess scales that overlap the edge of the cover circle.

Use a frilling tool to indent the line for the spines. On the covers where the legs are going to be placed, press the leg lightly into the scales to make a slight indent and lift it away again. This will help the leg adhere more securely to the cover when it is attached.

9 Cut and add spines. Thinly roll out golden ochre icing and use a sharp knife to cut the dragon's spines. You can do this freehand — they are just a series of small, slightly curved triangles, graduating in size from the end of the tail.

Attach the spines to the cover discs, placing them flat along the side of the body, gradually standing them upright in the marked indent where the spine twists, then laying them flat along the edge again.

10 Cover cupcakes. Brush the 14 ganached cupcakes with syrup and attach the decorated covers (plus the remaining plain black cover for the head).

Mix brown colour paste with alcohol to a rich caramel colour, then wash and paint the tips of the spines to give them added definition.

Disc for dragon's head.

Colour the tips of the dragon's spines with a caramel colour.

11 Attach head. Very gently position the prepared head on the remaining plain cupcake and attach with a dab of water. For the horns, cut two pieces of wire and mould some thinly rolled yellow icing around one end of each piece, as shown, leaving some wire extending for inserting the horns into the head. Brush a tiny dab of water onto the end of the horn where it will contact the head, and gently push the ends of the wires into the head.

Attach dragon's head to disc.

Roll yellow icing around wire inserts. and attach horns to head.

12 Attach legs. Using a fine paintbrush, carefully dab a little water along the curved inner edge of the wire-supported legs and gently insert the wires into the edge of the appropriate cupcakes. Dab water onto the underside of the near-side legs (that do not have wire supports) and position them in the indents on the cupcakes. If you are having trouble getting these unsupported legs to stay in place, you may need to 'glue' them in position with a small dab of royal icing instead of water.

Insert legs into cupcakes using a dab of water to hold them in place.

13 Arrange cupcakes. Assemble the finished cupcakes in their correct positions on a cake board. Wow!

Painting & piping

So you've mastered some pretty wonderful cupcakes. Now it's time to add a couple of extra creative techniques to your repertoire. Painting and piping might seem tricky at first, but the secret is to practise till you feel confident. It's certainly worth the effort because the results are spectacular and will take your cupcakes to the next level.

Animal prints

Although these cupcakes might look complicated, they are actually really fun and easy to make. They are a great introduction to the art of airbrushing because animal patterns are organic and uneven, so it is difficult to make a mistake.

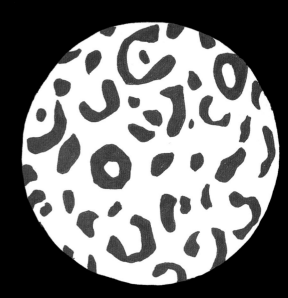

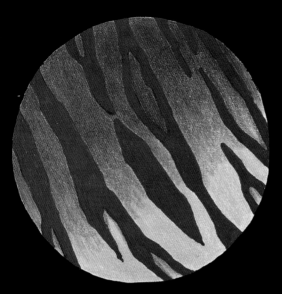

Materials

6 ganached cupcakes
100 ml (3½ fl oz) syrup
Cornflour in shaker
250 g (9 oz) fondant icing
Colour paste: black,
    brown, orange
Cake-decorating alcohol
Airbrush colour: yellow,
    orange, brown

Equipment

Large and small rolling pins
Cranked palette knife
Small sharp kitchen knife
Flexi-smoother
Pastry brush
Fine and medium paintbrushes
Circle cutters
Airbrush machine
Thin cardboard, for mask
Pencil and scissors

Techniques checklist

Recipes (page 204)
Ganaching cupcakes (page 208)
Colouring fondant icing
    (page 210)
Covering cupcakes (page 209)
Airbrushing (page 216)
Edible painting and colour wash
    (page 213)

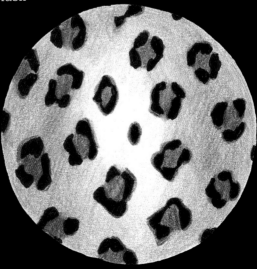

Conversation cupcakes

We designed our conversation cupcakes so that you can create any message you want: 'I love you', 'Get well soon'… It's a sweet way to show someone you care. To create your own message, choose a font and words on the computer, but be sure to check that they will fit on the speech bubble.

Materials

12 cupcakes, trimmed fairly flat, and ganached
125 ml (4 fl oz/½ cup) syrup
Cornflour in shaker
1 kg (2 lb 4 oz) fondant icing
Colour paste: blue, purple, black, red, green, brown, yellow, orange, teal, white-white (or colours of your choice)
Cake-decorating alcohol
About 300 g (10½ oz) royal icing

Equipment

2B pencil, fine tip pen, A3 paper and tracing paper
Large and small rolling pins
Cranked palette knife
Small sharp kitchen knife
Flexi-smoother
Pastry brush
Fine and medium paintbrushes
Piping bag
No. 1 or No. 2 piping tip
Circle cutters
Cutters of various other shapes
50 cm (20 in) square cake board (optional)
Paint palette

Techniques checklist

Step-by-step

1 **Make templates.** Use the speech bubble outlines on pages 108 and 109 to make the templates. You can also use cutters to trace basic shapes, such as hearts, circles and flowers, stretching them, if desired, to create even more shapes. To make a template of your message, write the words freehand or print them from a computer in a font that appeals. Remember to trace them back-to-front onto the speech bubble template so that they will be the right way round when transferred to the icing.

2 **Colour fondant icing.** Mix the colours the day before if possible, to make intense colours easier to work with. You should allow about 40 g (1½ oz) per cupcake for each cover and about 20 g (¾ oz) of each of two contrasting colours for a speech bubble.

3 **Colour royal icing.** Use colours of your choice to colour the royal icing and cover it tightly with plastic wrap until ready to use. Only a small amount of each colour will be required — enough to fill one-third of a piping bag. We used white, yellow, blue, green, black and pink, but the choice of colours is really up to you.

4 **Cover cupcakes.** Cover the 12 ganached cupcakes in different colours, as shown, allowing about 40 g (1½ oz) fondant icing per cupcake.

5 **Decorate cupcakes.**

SPEECH BUBBLES Roll out coloured fondant icing to about 2 mm (¹⁄₁₆ in) thick and, using a speech bubble template, transfer the pattern to the icing. Using a sharp knife, cut out the speech bubble (alternatively, use different shaped cutters), smooth the outer edges with your finger and cover it with plastic wrap to prevent it drying out. Roll out icing of a contrasting colour and adhere the cut-out speech bubble to the rolled icing with a dab of water. Using a sharp knife, cut around the shape again, leaving a border between 3 mm (⅛ in) and 6 mm (¼ in) wide. It's best at this point to transfer the message words to the top speech bubble as well, to use as a guide for piping.

Attach the completed speech bubbles to the top of the cupcakes with a dab of water. (Do not be tempted to pipe onto the speech bubble before adhering it to the top of the cupcake. Royal icing dries hard and is likely to crack if you attempt to bend it while smoothing the speech bubble onto the cake.)

Shapes can be stretched into other shapes.

Templates or cutters can be used for shapes.

Attach to contrasting icing colour.

Roll out icing and cut shape.

Cut around shape, leaving a contrasting border.

Cut speech bubbles freehand, or use templates.

Attach speech bubbles to prepared cupcakes.

PIPING THE MESSAGE Using a No. 1 or No. 2 tip, practise piping royal icing on scrap fondant icing or even on the benchtop until you feel confident enough to pipe on top of a speech bubble.

When you are ready, the most economical way to work is to pipe all the words of a particular colour at the same time.

If you have transferred the message to the top of the speech bubble, try to pipe as accurately as possible over the pencil lines to make sure they no longer remain visible.

For some finer writing, such as Chinese, Arabic and Hindi, it may be easier to paint the message using colour paste mixed with alcohol, rather than trying to pipe it accurately.

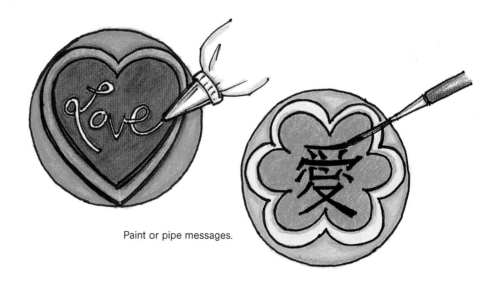

Paint or pipe messages.

Amigurumi family

These 'knitted' characters were inspired by amigurumi, which is the Japanese art of knitting or crocheting small stuffed animals and little creatures. They are a great introduction to piping, as they are simple to make and very effective.

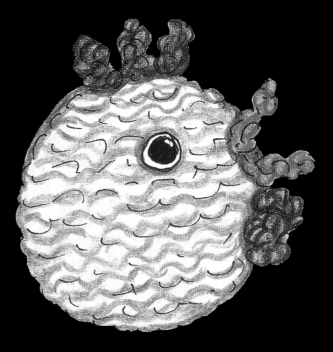

Materials

6 ganached cupcakes
100 ml (3½ fl oz) syrup
Cornflour in shaker
250 g (9 oz) fondant icing
Colour paste: blue, purple, black,
    red, green, brown, yellow,
    orange, white-white
Cake-decorating alcohol
About 600 g (1 lb 5 oz) royal icing
Dried spaghetti
Piping gel
6 pink flat-back acrylic
    diamantes (used by
    dressmakers)

Equipment

Large and small rolling pins
Cranked palette knife
Small sharp kitchen knife
Flexi-smoother
Pastry brush
Frilling tool
Small balling tool
Piping bags
No. 1, No. 2, No. 3 and No. 4
    piping tips
Fine and medium paintbrushes
Circle cutters
Small piece of linen or other
    coarse fabric
50 cm (20 in) square cake board
    (optional)

Techniques checklist

Recipes (page 204)
Ganaching cupcakes (page 208)
Colouring fondant icing
    page 210)
Red and black icing (page 211)
Covering cupcakes (page 209)
Piping with royal icing
    (page 217)
Eyes (page 215)

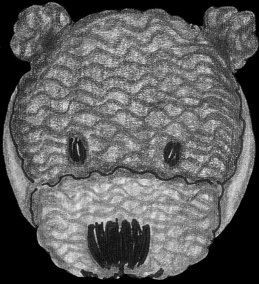

Step-by-step

1 Colour fondant icing. Mix the colours the day before if possible, to make intense colours easier to work with. You can use any colour for the covers, including skin-coloured icing, if desired, for the faces. You will need about 40 g (1½ oz) icing for each cupcake, as well as very small amounts of leftover icing for decorative features, such as buttons, bows, black eyes, and so on.

2 Colour royal icing. Only a small amount of each colour is required — enough to fill one-third of a piping bag. To reproduce the cupcakes pictured, you will need to make white, yellow, blue, red, green, orange, black, brown and purple royal icing. Keep the icing tightly covered with plastic wrap until ready to use.

3 Cover cupcakes. Cover the six ganached cupcakes in different colours, using the photograph as a guide, or choose your own colours. If making the amigurumi people, it is best to cover the cupcakes in skin-coloured icing just before you are ready to decorate them, as the covers should be soft enough to imprint with a fabric pattern (see page 118).

4 Decorate cupcakes.

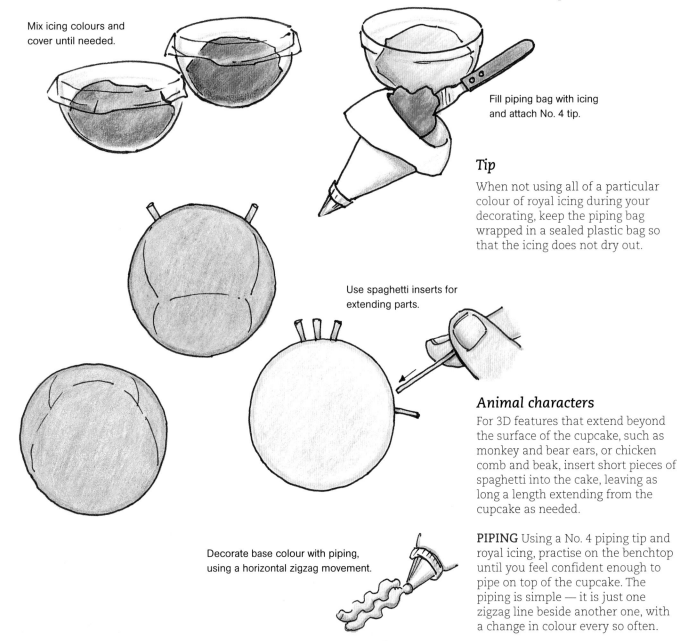

Mix icing colours and cover until needed.

Fill piping bag with icing and attach No. 4 tip.

Tip

When not using all of a particular colour of royal icing during your decorating, keep the piping bag wrapped in a sealed plastic bag so that the icing does not dry out.

Use spaghetti inserts for extending parts.

Animal characters

For 3D features that extend beyond the surface of the cupcake, such as monkey and bear ears, or chicken comb and beak, insert short pieces of spaghetti into the cake, leaving as long a length extending from the cupcake as needed.

Decorate base colour with piping, using a horizontal zigzag movement.

PIPING Using a No. 4 piping tip and royal icing, practise on the benchtop until you feel confident enough to pipe on top of the cupcake. The piping is simple — it is just one zigzag line beside another one, with a change in colour every so often.

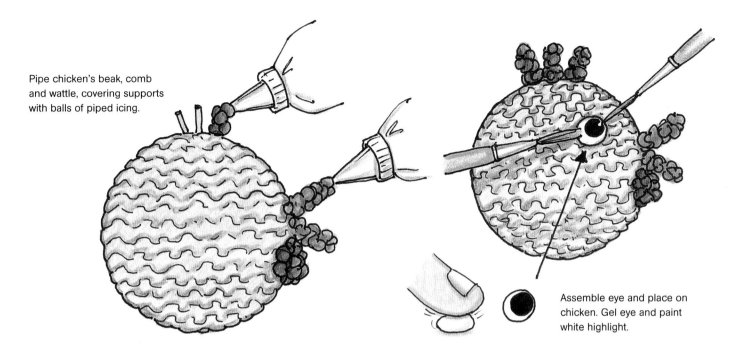

Pipe chicken's beak, comb and wattle, covering supports with balls of piped icing.

Assemble eye and place on chicken. Gel eye and paint white highlight.

CHICKEN Cover the cupcake with lines of piping in yellow base colour. To add the wattle and comb, change to red royal icing and pipe dots of colour over the extending spaghetti supports, until they are completely covered. Using orange, cover the beak in the same way.

For the eyes, roll a small ball of white fondant icing, about 8 mm ($^{3}/_{8}$ in) diameter, and press flat to about 12 mm ($^{1}/_{2}$ in).

Roll and press a smaller black pupil in the same way and stick the pupil to the white circle with a dab of water. Attach the eye to the chicken with water, paint the eye with piping gel and, when dry, finish with a white-white colour paste highlight.

BEAR AND MONKEY Using the illustration and photograph as a guide, pipe these animals in the same way as the chicken, using royal icing in appropriate colours and covering the extending spaghetti supports, as before. Using black royal icing and a No. 2 tip, pipe on noses, eyes and mouths, as shown.

Pipe bear and monkey in same way as chicken.

Pipe on eyes, noses and mouths with a No. 2 piping tip.

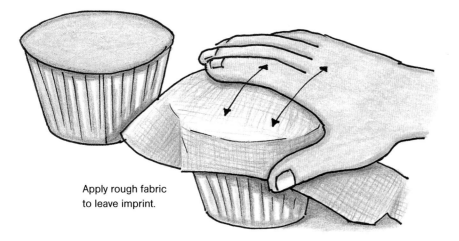

Apply rough fabric
to leave imprint.

Cover cupcakes and smooth.

Amigurumi family

FACES While the fondant icing cover is still soft, place a small piece of linen or other coarse fabric over the cover and rub gently to imprint the icing with the fabric pattern, to give the impression that the people are actually made from cloth, like a soft toy.

Using the diagram as a guide to placement for adults and children, indent the eye sockets and mouths with a balling tool and frilling tool respectively. Roll small balls of black icing and adhere to the eye sockets with a dab of water.

Pipe the mouths using a No. 1 piping tip. Insert spaghetti supports into grandpa's head and pipe the ears with a No. 3 tip. Pipe the nose at the same time.

Paint the eyes with piping gel and, when dry, pipe on tiny white highlights with a No. 1 piping tip, drawing three fine icing threads from the centre of the eye, as shown.

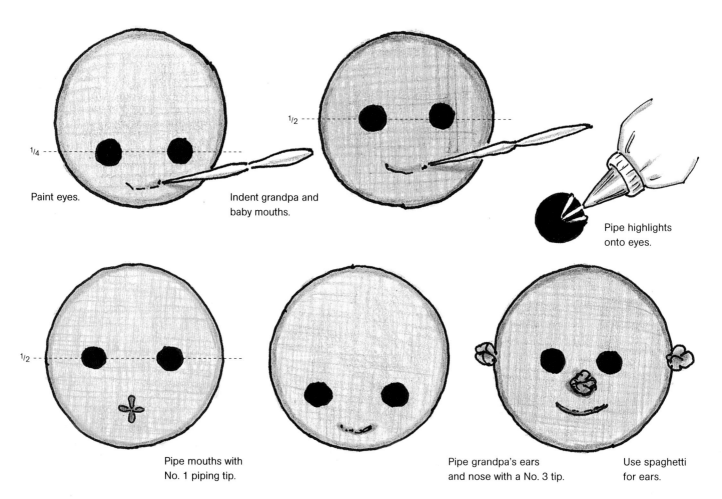

Paint eyes.

Indent grandpa and baby mouths.

Pipe highlights onto eyes.

Pipe mouths with No. 1 piping tip.

Pipe grandpa's ears and nose with a No. 3 tip.

Use spaghetti for ears.

HATS Pipe the hats onto the cupcakes in the colours of your choice, using a No. 4 tip and the same zigzag piping technique as used for the animals.

Pipe hats onto all three cupcakes.

Squash pea-sized ball of fondant icing.

Mark details with frilling tool.

Use No. 1 piping tip for thread.

Cut and fold tails for bow.

BUTTONS AND BOWS To make a bow for the hat, roll fondant icing out thinly, cut two shaped strips, as shown, and fold into a bow with trailing ends, following the diagrams.

To make a button, squash a pea-sized ball of fondant icing into a flat circle. Mark the inner moulding and holes with a frilling tool. Use a No. 1 piping tip to pipe the threads holding the button in place. Adhere these decorations to the completed cupcakes with a dab of water.

To make bow, cut two pieces of fondant icing.

Place tails over folded bow.

Secure tails to bow with small piece of fondant icing.

Mark bow details with frilling tool.

HAIR Pipe tufts of hair peeping from beneath the hats, as well as grandpa's moustache, using a No. 3 piping tip and the colour of your choice.

Pipe hair using No. 3 piping tip. Add pink diamantes to cheeks with a dab of gel.

FINISHING Glue pink diamantes to the people's cheeks, using a dab of piping gel. (Do not add diamantes if the cupcakes are for children.)

Modelling

In this chapter, all of our decorating techniques are combined to make little works of art that will utterly delight your friends and family. It's hard to believe that all these exquisite creations are simply made from sugar, but if you can roll a ball, you can make a model. It's just a matter of knowing where to start. Begin with the basics, take your time and have fun; if you make a mistake, you can simply begin again — or eat it!

Playful puppies

This fun cupcake story was inspired by my chihuahua, Minky. However don't feel limited; with the same techniques you can re-create your own gorgeous pooch. This story needs to be as interactive as possible, so be sure to include any other mischief you can think of.

Materials

1 plain cupcake and 6 ganached
    cupcakes
100 ml (3½ fl oz) syrup
Cornflour in shaker
1 kg (2 lb 4 oz) fondant icing
Tylose powder
Colour paste: blue, red, pink,
    teal, purple, black, green,
    brown, yellow, orange,
    white-white
Airbrush colour: brown, yellow,
    orange
Cake-decorating alcohol
Small amount royal icing
Red and pink petal dust
Piping gel

Equipment

Large and small rolling pins
Cranked palette knife
Small sharp kitchen knife
Pastry brush
Flexi-smoother
Frilling tool
Fine and medium paintbrushes
Piping bag
No. 2 and No. 3 piping tips
Leaf piping tip (optional)
Circle cutters
Petal cutter and vein mould
    (optional)
Teacup and saucer mould
    (see page 220)
22-gauge florist's wire (or dried
    spaghetti, if for children)
Toothpicks or thin bamboo
    skewers, for support
Airbrush machine
Glue gun
Scissors (optional)

Techniques checklist

Recipes (page 204)
Ganaching cupcakes (page 208)
Colouring fondant icing
    (page 210)
Covering cupcakes (page 209)
Red and black icing (page 211)
Edible painting and colour wash
    (page 213)
Figurine modelling (page 218)
Making simple moulds
    (page 220)
Blush (page 214)
Eyes (page 215)
Gelling (page 213)

Step-by-step

1 Colour fondant icing. Mix the colours the day before if possible, to make the intense colours easier to work with. You will need about 40 g (1½ oz) icing per cupcake in the colours of your choice for the covers. (We used teal, green, terracotta, purple, red and brown.) You will also need 200 g (7 oz) white, 70 g (2½ oz) each of dark brown, light brown, terracotta and yellow, as well as small amounts of red, pink, hot-pink, purple, blue, orange and black.

2 Cover cupcakes. Using the colours of your choice, cover the 6 ganached cupcakes, allowing about 40 g (1½ oz) icing per cupcake. Reserve the plain cupcake for the puppy on its back.

3 Make figurines.

Note Before making each of the following models, knead a little Tylose powder into the icing for extra hardness.

Puppy on its back

COVER Trim the top of the plain cupcake so that it is slightly raised above the paper case but flat on top. Ganache cake and cover with white fondant icing. This is the puppy's body. The head will take up half the diameter of the cupcake. Mark the buttocks with a frilling tool, as shown. All the rest of the puppy's body parts are made from white icing.

HEAD AND LIMBS For the head, roll out a flattish ball of icing, about 12 mm (½ in) thick, that will take up the top half of the cupcake. Indent eye sockets just above the halfway point of the head. Make a pair of ears, smooth them with your fingers, indent with a frilling tool and insert spaghetti or wire supports. Roll a tail and insert a support as shown. Shape two front paws from small balls and mark the toes with a frilling tool. For the back feet, shape two rounded ovals that will take up the lower half of the cupcake.

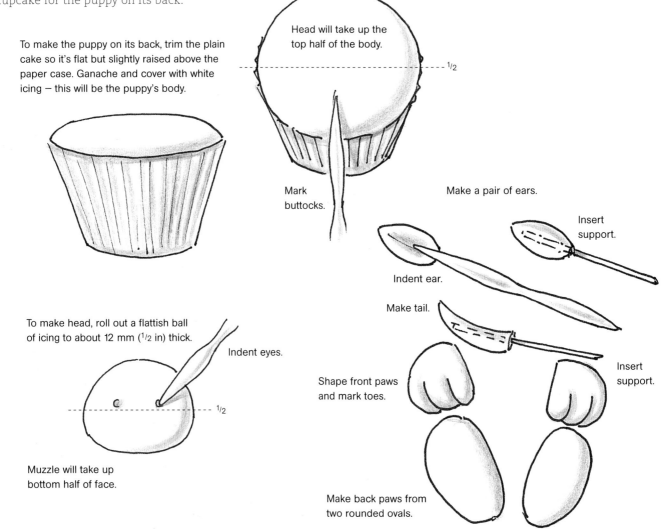

To make the puppy on its back, trim the plain cake so it's flat but slightly raised above the paper case. Ganache and cover with white icing – this will be the puppy's body.

Head will take up the top half of the body.

½

Mark buttocks.

Make a pair of ears.

Insert support.

Indent ear.

Make tail.

Insert support.

To make head, roll out a flattish ball of icing to about 12 mm (½ in) thick.

Indent eyes.

½

Muzzle will take up bottom half of face.

Shape front paws and mark toes.

Make back paws from two rounded ovals.

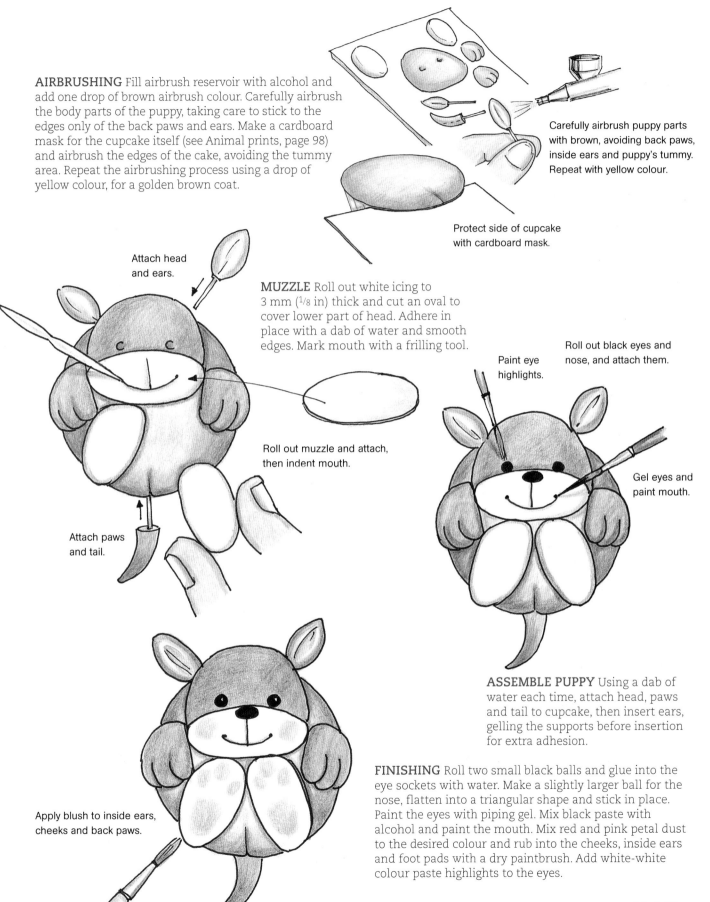

AIRBRUSHING Fill airbrush reservoir with alcohol and add one drop of brown airbrush colour. Carefully airbrush the body parts of the puppy, taking care to stick to the edges only of the back paws and ears. Make a cardboard mask for the cupcake itself (see Animal prints, page 98) and airbrush the edges of the cake, avoiding the tummy area. Repeat the airbrushing process using a drop of yellow colour, for a golden brown coat.

Carefully airbrush puppy parts with brown, avoiding back paws, inside ears and puppy's tummy. Repeat with yellow colour.

Protect side of cupcake with cardboard mask.

Attach head and ears.

MUZZLE Roll out white icing to 3 mm (1/8 in) thick and cut an oval to cover lower part of head. Adhere in place with a dab of water and smooth edges. Mark mouth with a frilling tool.

Roll out muzzle and attach, then indent mouth.

Attach paws and tail.

Paint eye highlights.

Roll out black eyes and nose, and attach them.

Gel eyes and paint mouth.

ASSEMBLE PUPPY Using a dab of water each time, attach head, paws and tail to cupcake, then insert ears, gelling the supports before insertion for extra adhesion.

Apply blush to inside ears, cheeks and back paws.

FINISHING Roll two small black balls and glue into the eye sockets with water. Make a slightly larger ball for the nose, flatten into a triangular shape and stick in place. Paint the eyes with piping gel. Mix black paste with alcohol and paint the mouth. Mix red and pink petal dust to the desired colour and rub into the cheeks, inside ears and foot pads with a dry paintbrush. Add white-white colour paste highlights to the eyes.

Modelling 127

Make and paint cup, and assemble teacup and saucer. Insert skewer to support puppy's head.

Puppy in a teacup

CUP AND SAUCER Make and assemble a teacup and saucer (see Fairy tea party, page 167). Paint a flower detail on the side of the cup before assembling the cup and saucer. Insert a gelled support skewer through the completed set, then insert the bottom end into the cake to secure the cup and saucer, and leave a length extending above the cup, long enough to reach through the puppy's body and into its head.

PUPPY Shape light brown icing into head and body, as shown. Roll a ball of white icing, squash slightly and shape into the puppy's muzzle, tapering all sides to a fine edge, except the nose area. Attach to the head with a dab of water. Use a frilling tool to indent the mouth and eye sockets.

From thinly rolled, light brown icing and pink icing, cut out two ears and two smaller inner ears, respectively. Adhere inner ears to outer ears, smooth, and insert supports.

Roll and apply eyes and nose as for puppy on its back (see page 127 for eye/nose instruction). Mix black colour paste with alcohol and paint in the mouth with a fine paintbrush. Paint the eyes with piping gel and allow to dry.

Dab water on the underneath of the puppy's body and gently lower the body onto the skewer, pushing it carefully through the body and then into the head. Push the ear supports into the head, adding a dab of water where the two meet. Roll little front legs from light brown icing, as shown. Mark paws with a frilling tool and attach legs to body with a dab of water. Curl the paws over the front of the teacup. Finish each eye with a white-white colour paste highlight.

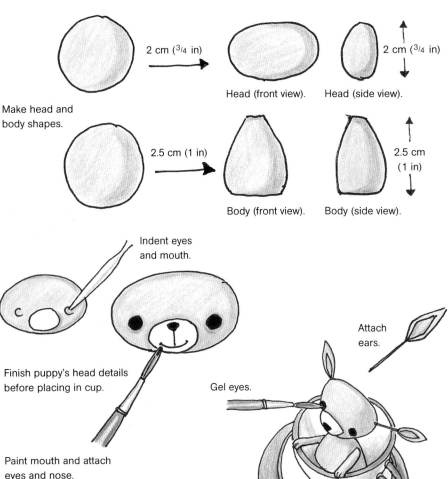

Make head and body shapes.

2 cm (³/₄ in)

Head (front view).

2 cm (³/₄ in)

Head (side view).

2.5 cm (1 in)

Body (front view).

2.5 cm (1 in)

Body (side view).

Indent eyes and mouth.

Finish puppy's head details before placing in cup.

Paint mouth and attach eyes and nose.

Make front legs and attach.

2 cm (³/₄ in)

Gel eyes.

Attach ears.

Paint eye highlights.

Assemble figurine – give the puppy a quirky look by attaching the head on a slight angle.

Puppy with a toilet roll

PUPPY Shape dark brown icing into head and body, as shown. Slightly flatten the back of the head and trim away a little on the front edge of the neck so that the head will sit at an angle. Adhere head to body with a dab of water. Push a gelled support skewer into a covered cupcake, leaving enough extending above the cover to insert through the puppy's body and into its head. Indent the eye sockets with a frilling tool.

From dark brown icing, roll front legs, tail and back paws, marking toes with a frilling tool before adhering the parts to the body with a dab of water. From thinly rolled, dark-brown icing and pink icing, make ears as for Puppy in a teacup (opposite).

FOR THE MUZZLE Thinly roll light brown icing and cover the dog's snout from just under the eyes, smoothing the icing over the top and front of the muzzle, gathering excess under chin. Trim excess away and smooth under chin with your fingers. Indent the mouth with a frilling tool.

Make and adhere eyes and nose, as for puppy on its back (see page 127). Mix black colour paste with alcohol and paint in the mouth and whisker freckles with a fine paintbrush. Paint the eyes with piping gel and allow to dry.

2.5 cm (1 in) — Head (front view). — Head (side view). — 3 cm (1¼ in) — Make head and body shapes. Then make tail, front legs and back paws.

3.25 cm (1¼ in) — Body (front view). — Body (side view). — 4 cm (1½ in)

2.5 cm (1 in) — Mark paws.

1/2 — Indent eyes.

Cut out ears. — Smooth and shape ears, and insert support.

Secure with support stick.

Roll brown icing into a sausage.

Roll a white icing strip around the sausage.

Cover puppy's muzzle from just under eyes with light brown icing.

Trim excess and smooth under chin.

Paint mouth and whisker freckles.

Add eye highlights.

TOILET PAPER Roll a brown icing sausage, as shown, and indent each end with the frilling tool to give the appearance of a hollow tube. Roll a strip of white icing around the tube and trim off excess when wrapped.

Roll out white icing as thinly as possible and cut 1.5 cm-wide (⅝ in) strips. Apply to cupcake in soft folds, adhering one fold into the mouth indent as shown. Add white-white colour paste highlights to the eyes.

Sunflower puppy

FLOWERPOT Take a golf ball-sized piece of terracotta icing and roll a cylinder, slightly tapered at one end, as shown. Cut a pot shape from the cylinder and smooth with your fingers. Roll out dark brown icing thinly, cut a circle the same size as the diameter of the pot top and adhere to top of pot. Roll a thin strip of terracotta icing and cut a rim for the pot. Attach to top of pot, leaving a lip extending slightly above the brown 'earth'. Cut the ends of the strip flush so they join perfectly.

PUPPY Shape golden-brown icing into puppy's shoulders and head. Indent eye sockets with a frilling tool. Insert a gelled support stick into the flowerpot, leaving enough extending to pass through the puppy's shoulders and into the head. Apply a dab of water to parts that are going to touch and position shoulders and head on extending support skewer. Make and insert ears, as for Puppy on its back (see page 127). Roll out white icing thinly and cut and apply a muzzle, as for Puppy with a toilet roll (see page 129).

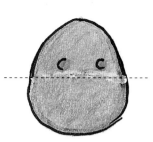

Indent eyes just above muzzle line.

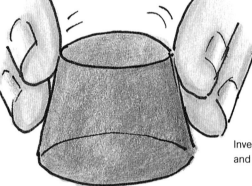

Roll terracotta icing and cut a pot shape 3 cm (1¼ in) diameter across base and 4 cm (1½ in) across top.

Invert pot shape and smooth.

Cut out dark brown circle to fit top of pot, and attach.

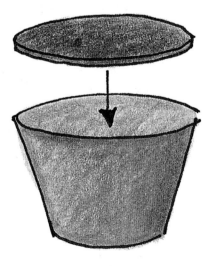

Cut out trim for pot.

Attach trim around top, creating a lip.

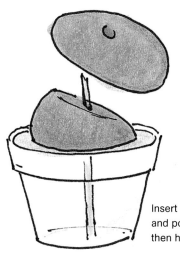

Insert support skewer, and position shoulders, then head.

Cover puppy's muzzle from just under eyes with white icing. Smooth icing over top and front of snout until it gathers under chin. Trim excess.

PETALS Roll out yellow icing to 2 mm (1/16 in) thick and cut out petals, using a petal cutter or a knife. Use a vein mould or a frilling tool to make veins on each petal. Insert a support wire into each petal, leaving a length extending for insertion into the puppy's head.

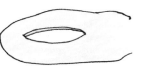

Roll out yellow icing.

Use petal cutter or knife to cut out petals.

Use vein mould or frilling tool to mark veins, then insert support wire.

AIRBRUSHING Fill airbrush reservoir with alcohol and one drop of orange airbrush colour and airbrush the lower part of each petal.

Airbrush orange colour on lower parts of petals.

Paint eye highlights.

Insert petals, attach eyes and nose. Gel eyes.

FINISHING Roll and adhere eyes and nose, as for Puppy on its back (see page 127). Paint eyes with piping gel, mark mouth with a frilling tool and apply blush to muzzle. Carefully insert petals around head. With a dab of water, position the flowerpot on a green-covered cupcake, pushing pot into cover a little. Using a No. 3 piping tip or a leaf tip, pipe small blades of grass around the lower edge of the pot. Mix black colour paste with alcohol to paint puppy's mouth, and add white-white colour paste highlights to eyes.

Paint mouth.

Mark mouth and apply blush.

Attach pot to cupcake. Then pipe leaves at base of pot.

Sleeping puppy

PUPPY BODY Roll out a longish sausage of white icing, tapering it at each end. The back section of the puppy should be about 5.5 cm (2¼ in) long. Bend tapered ends around to form legs, as shown, and shape body contours and leg outlines with a frilling tool. Use a small, sharp knife to separate legs, then use your fingers to smooth them into rounded shapes. Using a dab of water, attach the puppy's body to a covered cupcake. Thinly roll out light brown icing and cut random-shaped patches. Adhere to body with a dab of water. Cut and construct ears as for Puppy in a teacup (see page 128). From light brown icing, roll a tapered sausage for a tail and insert a support wire. Roll out purple icing thinly and cut a circle with a diameter just slightly larger than the neck. From purple scraps, cut two ribbon shapes. Attach ribbons to neck with a dab of water and attach the circle in the same way.

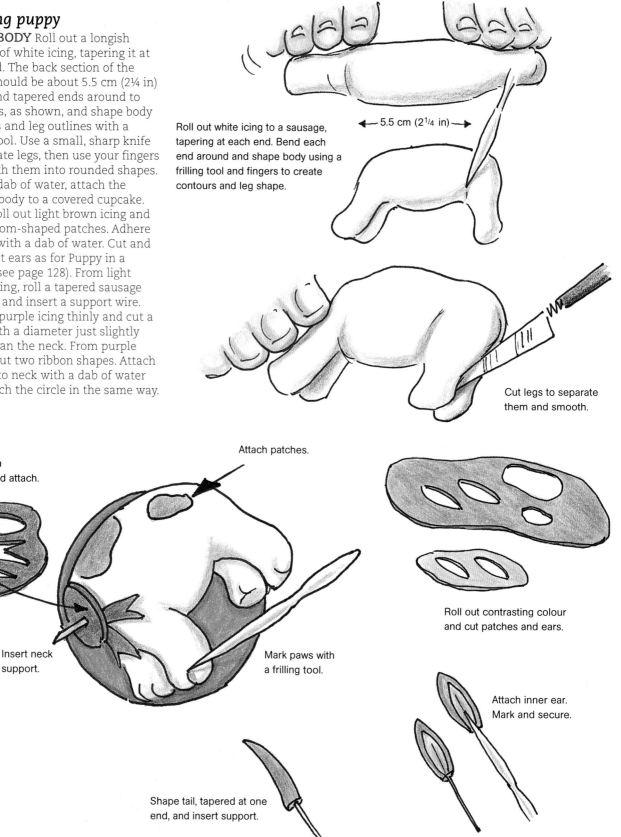

Roll out white icing to a sausage, tapering at each end. Bend each end around and shape body using a frilling tool and fingers to create contours and leg shape.

←— 5.5 cm (2¼ in) —→

Cut legs to separate them and smooth.

Cut ribbon shapes and attach.

Attach patches.

Insert neck support.

Mark paws with a frilling tool.

Roll out contrasting colour and cut patches and ears.

Shape tail, tapered at one end, and insert support.

Attach inner ear. Mark and secure.

PUPPY HEAD Roll light brown icing into a flattened ball for the head, as shown. For the muzzle, roll and slightly flatten two pea-sized balls of white icing and attach to the head. Push a gelled support skewer into the body through the centre of the purple circle, leaving a length extending to support the head. With a dab of water, gently push the head onto the support stick, and insert ears and tail.

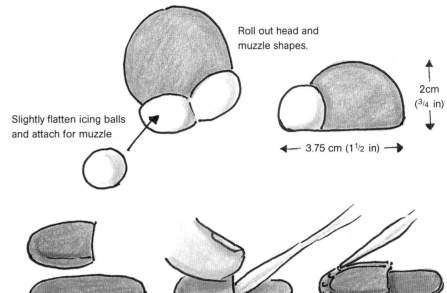

Roll out head and muzzle shapes.

2cm (³⁄₄ in)

← 3.75 cm (1¹⁄₂ in) →

Slightly flatten icing balls and attach for muzzle

SLIPPER Roll out hot-pink icing and cut shapes for the slipper, as shown. Attach upper to sole with a dab of water around the edges and insert frilling tool to make an opening for a foot. Crimp the edges of the upper and sole together with the frilling tool.

Shape slipper pieces from hot-pink icing and use the frilling tool to finish slipper.

FINISHING Roll black icing thinly and cut and adhere shapes for the nose and sleeping eyes. Rub petal dust into the cheeks and foot pads using a dry paintbrush. Gently lift the front leg and adhere the slipper under the paw. Mix black colour paste with alcohol and paint the toes and whisker freckles.

Insert tail.

Attach head and insert ears.

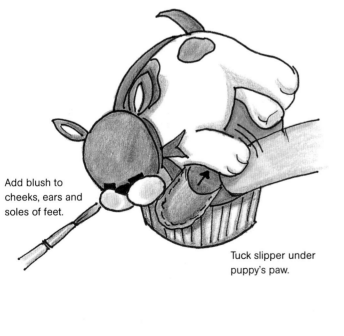

Add blush to cheeks, ears and soles of feet.

Tuck slipper under puppy's paw.

Make head and
body shapes.

Head (front view).   Head (side view).

2.5 cm
(1 in)

Secure puppy on
support, towards
back of cake.

Body (front view).   Body (side view).

3.75 cm
(1 3/8 in)

Puppy with a bone

Shape dark brown icing head, body,
tail and back legs, as shown. Mark
toes with a frilling tool. Push a gelled
skewer into a covered cupcake,
leaving an extension to push through
body and into head. Dab water on
areas that will touch, then gently
lower body and head onto skewer.
Attach back legs and tail. Roll, cut,
construct and attach ears as for
Puppy in a teacup (see page 128). For
the muzzle, roll a pea-sized ball of
light brown icing, flatten slightly and
adhere to face. Flatten a tiny ball of
the same colour and attach to the eye
area. Mark eye sockets and mouth.
Roll and shape an oversized bone
from white icing, and adhere to
cupcake. Roll and mark front paws
and attach to the body, resting the
paws on the bone. Make and finish
eyes and nose as for Puppy in a
teacup (see page 128).

1.5 cm (5/8 in)

Cut out ears, smooth and shape.

Mark eyes
and mouth.

View from above.

Shape and
attach muzzle.

Flatten small icing
ball for eye area.

2.5 cm (1 in)   Make back legs.

Roll out legs and shape
paws. Attach to body with
paws resting on bone.

Gel eyes, paint mouth
black and paint eye
highlights.

3 cm
(1 1/4 in)

Shape bone using
knife and fingers.

3 cm
(1 1/4 in)

6 cm
(2 1/2 in)

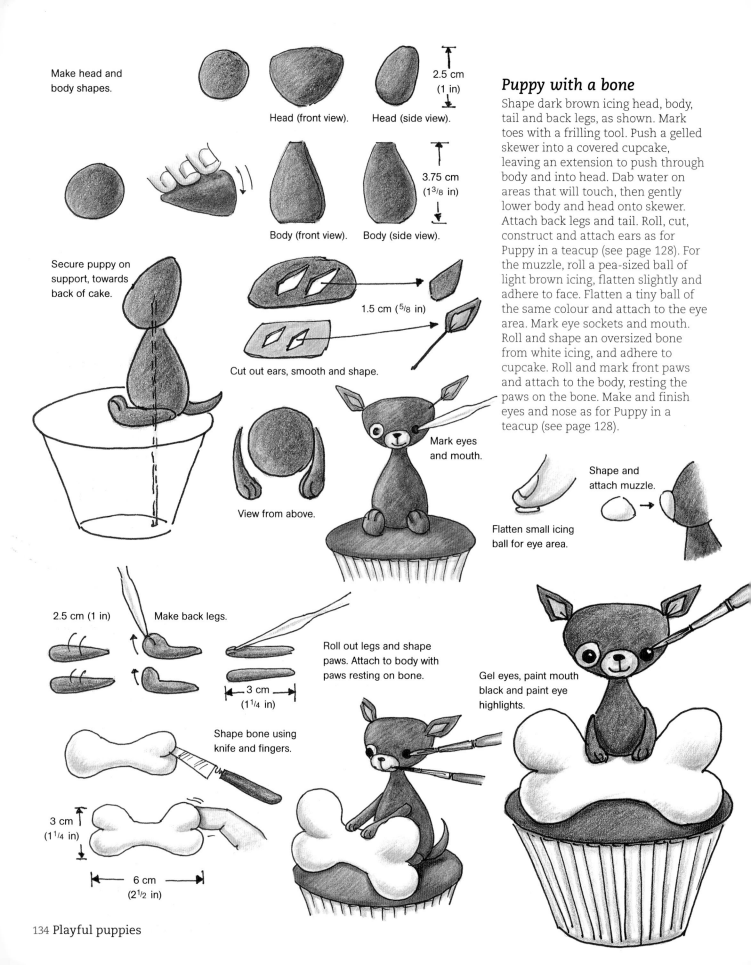

Puppy with a blanket

PUPPY Shape white icing into head and body, as shown. Push a gelled support skewer into a covered cupcake, leaving an extension to push through body and into head. Dab water on areas that will touch, then gently lower the body and head onto the support skewer. Roll and shape front and back legs, and tail, as shown. Adhere to body with a dab of water. Roll and flatten a small ball of black icing for the ear, smooth with your fingers and insert a wire support. Flatten a tiny black ball and apply to the eye area. Indent eye sockets and mark the muzzle and mouth with a frilling tool. Make and finish eyes and nose as for Puppy in a teacup (see page 128). Insert the ear.

BLANKET AND BOW Roll red icing thinly and cut a 17 cm x 6 cm (6½ x 2½ in) rectangle. Drape over the puppy, applying a little water to areas that touch. Cut and construct a bow (see page 119) and adhere.

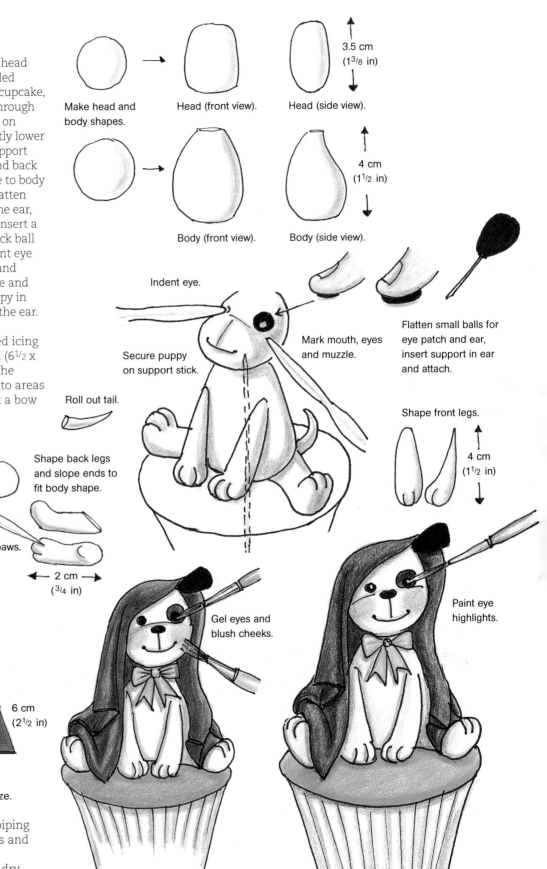

Make head and body shapes.

Head (front view).

Head (side view).

3.5 cm (1³⁄₈ in)

Body (front view).

Body (side view).

4 cm (1½ in)

Indent eye.

Secure puppy on support stick.

Mark mouth, eyes and muzzle.

Flatten small balls for eye patch and ear, insert support in ear and attach.

Roll out tail.

Shape front legs.

4 cm (1½ in)

Roll out eyes and nose, attach.

Shape back legs and slope ends to fit body shape.

Mark paws.

2 cm (³⁄₄ in)

6 cm (2½ in)

17 cm (6½ in)

For blanket, roll icing and trim to size.

FINISHING Paint eyes with piping gel, rub petal dust into cheeks and add white-white colour paste highlights to eyes, once gel is dry.

Gel eyes and blush cheeks.

Paint eye highlights.

The vegetable patch

I'm a huge fan of good-quality marzipan and believe that the best training for modern cake decorating lies in mastering traditional marzipan modelling techniques. The vegetable patch designs were inspired by traditional marzipan sweets popular in Europe, however, here they are made from rolled fondant icing so that they can be coloured brilliantly.

Materials

6 ganached cupcakes
100 ml ($3\frac{1}{2}$ fl oz) syrup
Cornflour in shaker
750 g (1 lb 10 oz) fondant icing
Colour paste: red, green, orange, brown, pink, purple, black, white-white
Airbrush colour: purple, red, orange, black, brown
Cake-decorating alcohol
Piping gel
Tylose powder
Edible silver lustre dust

Equipment

Large and small rolling pins
Cranked palette knife
Small sharp kitchen knife
Flexi-smoother
Pastry brush
Frilling tool
Synthetic scourer
Fine and medium paintbrushes
Circle cutters
Airbrush machine
Petal cutter and vein mould (optional)
No. 4 piping tip
Thin bamboo skewer
22-gauge florist's wire
Glue gun
Tracing wheel, from haberdashery stores (optional)
50 cm (20 in) square cake board (optional)

Techniques checklist

Recipes (page 204)
Ganaching cupcakes (page 208)
Colouring fondant icing (page 210)
Red and black icing (page 211)
Skin-coloured icing (page 211)
Marbling (page 212)
Covering cupcakes (page 209)
Figurine modelling (page 218)
Airbrushing (page 216)
Edible painting and colour wash (page 213)
Painting in silver or gold (page 214)

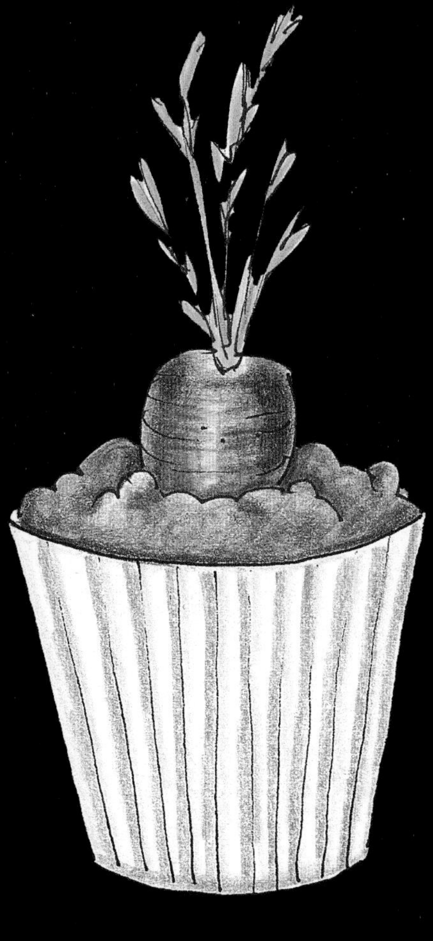

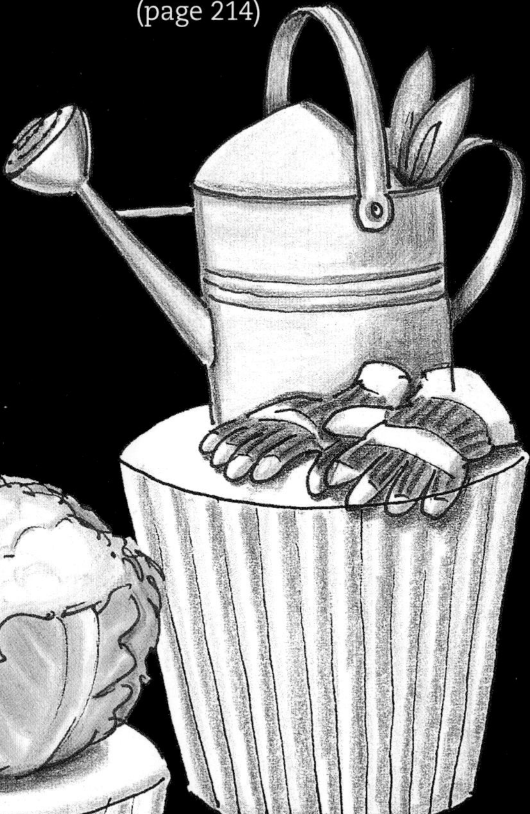

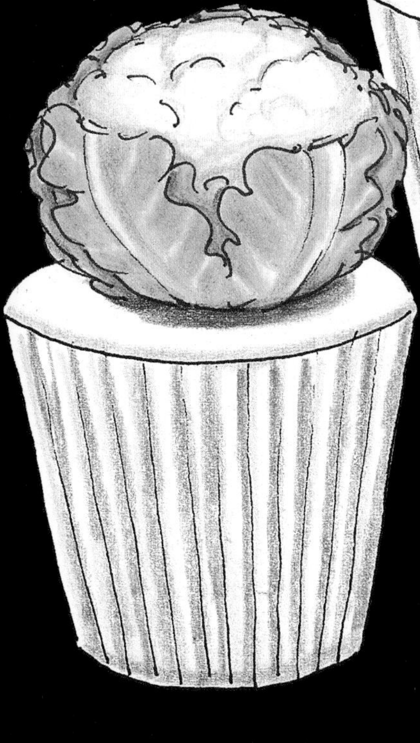

Step-by-step

1 Colour fondant icing. Mix the colours the day before if possible, to make the intense colours easier to work with. You will need about 160 g (5½ oz) grey/white marbled icing, and 40 g (1½ oz) each of bright green and dark brown, for the covers. You will also need small amounts of pink skin-coloured, red, grey, white, purple, orange, dark green, light green, dark brown and light brown.

2 Cover cupcakes. Using our colours, or the colours of your choice, cover the ganached cupcakes, allowing about 40 g (1½ oz) icing per cupcake.

3 Make decorations.

Vegetables: basic shapes

Before making each of the following models, knead a little Tylose powder into the icing for extra hardness.

PUMPKIN Roll about 100 g (3½ oz) pink skin-coloured icing into a ball, squash slightly to flatten top and bottom and indent the sides with frilling tool. Adhere a couple of tiny flattened buttons of skin-coloured icing on top for the stalk remnants.

TOMATO Roll about 80 g (2¾ oz) red icing into a ball, squash the ball slightly to give it a plump, round shape, lightly score the sides with your frilling tool to shape and make an indentation in the top.

EGGPLANT (AUBERGINE) Roll about 45 g (1½ oz) purple icing into a ball, then elongate slightly to create the shape of an eggplant. Indent bottom stalk with a frilling tool.

CARROT Roll about 20 g (¾ oz) orange icing into a short cylinder, then elongate it slightly, leaving it domed on top and flat across the bottom. Use the frilling tool to mark horizontal lines around the sides.

CAULIFLOWER Roll about 55 g (2 oz) white icing into a ball. Use a frilling tool to separate the surface into florets, then rough up the florets with a clean, synthetic scourer.

Vegetables: airbrushing and painting

Fill the airbrush reservoir with alcohol and one drop of the appropriate colour and airbrush the tomato, carrot and eggplant. You may need several layers of different colours to get the depth and correct colour for each of the vegetables. Use real vegetables or photographs as a reference. Paint or airbrush the pumpkin, depending on the variety you have chosen to model and paint the remnant stalk brown. Mix up colour paste and alcohol and colour wash the cauliflower with a slightly darker wash to add a little depth to the florets. Paint dark and light horizontal lines around the carrot after airbrushing.

Make all the vegetable shapes.

Shape pumpkin, mark with frilling tool, and add stalk remnants.

Shape eggplant and mark with frilling tool.

Shape tomato and mark with frilling tool.

Shape carrot top and mark with frilling tool.

Use frilling tool and synthetic scourer to make cauliflower florets.

Airbrush and/or paint all the vegetables and fruit, as described, before attaching leaves.

Stalks and leaves

TOMATO Shape a pea-sized piece of dark green icing into a stalk and insert a wire support. Cut a star-shaped calyx from thinly rolled dark green icing, and pinch the tips of the star to make them pointy. Fix the calyx to the top of the tomato with a dab of water, push the stem support through the centre and curl up the ends of the calyx, as shown. Colour wash with a lighter green colour in places, to make it more realistic.

EGGPLANT (AUBERGINE) Shape a pea-sized piece of light green icing into a stalk and insert a wire support. Cut a four-leafed calyx from thinly rolled light green icing, make a hole in the centre and adhere to the eggplant with a dab of water. Push the stem support through the centre hole and curl the ends of the calyx away from eggplant a little. Brush with a brown wash.

CARROT Shape about 15 g ($^1/_2$ oz) bright green icing into a short sausage and insert a support wire into one end. Use a knife to cut the other end into strips, adding extra markings with a frilling tool. Insert support wire into top of carrot and finish the stalk with a darker brownish-green colour wash around the base.

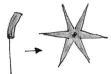

Make stalks, stems and leaves.

Insert wire into tomato stem.

Make tomato calyx.

Make eggplant calyx.

Insert wire into eggplant stem.

Make and attach carrot stems as described.

Cut out cauliflower leaves.

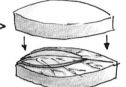

Mark veins with vein mould or frilling tool.

CAULIFLOWER Thinly roll out about 20 g ($^3/_4$ oz) light green icing. Use a petal cutter or small knife to cut 16 leaf shapes and mark the stem pattern with a vein mould or a frilling tool. Using a dab of water to secure each one, apply the leaves around the outside of the cauliflower, overlapping them slightly and curving them to the shape of the cauliflower. Apply a wash of darker green to the outer leaves, leaving the veins and inner leaves a lighter colour.

Secure leaves to cauliflower.

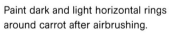

Paint dark and light horizontal rings around carrot after airbrushing.

Add a very light colour wash to add depth to cauliflower.

Refer to real vegetables and fruit for colours.

Watering can

DRUM Roll about 50 g (1¾ oz) grey icing into a slightly oval-shaped cylinder, about 4 cm (1½ in) long. Mark corrugations around the upper section of the drum with a frilling tool. Thinly roll out some more grey icing and cut a 3.5 cm-diameter (1⅜ in) circle. Trim away about one-third of this circle and place the remaining two-thirds on top of the cylinder, adhering the edges only, so that the centre curves up to form the cover. Dab the bottom of the cylinder with water, gently rest it on thinly rolled grey icing and cut around the base with a sharp knife, leaving a tiny rim. Roll a very thin grey rim for the top edge and adhere it around the top of the cylinder, cutting the edges flush and smoothing the join.

SPOUT AND HANDLES Cut two handles from thinly rolled grey icing and mould into shape. Allow these to dry a little, but attach them to the can with a dab of water before they are completely dry, so they can be adjusted to fit exactly but will hold their shape. Push the tip of a No. 4 piping tip onto the joins at each end of each handle, to mark the rivets.

Push a short length of wire into the drum just above the corrugations, then insert a skewer into the drum at a 45-degree angle, as shown. Glue-gun the wire to the skewer at their meeting point. Roll out a rectangle of grey icing for the spout, making it thicker at one end. Paint the skewer with water, then wrap the icing around it and trim excess, leaving the point of the skewer exposed. Wrap the support wire in a tiny amount of icing as well.

Mould a small disc for the watering rose, mark the holes with a frilling tool and a toothpick, and attach to the exposed end of the skewer.

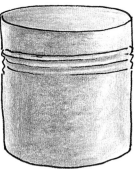

Roll slightly oval cylinder for watering can. Mark corrugations with frilling tool.

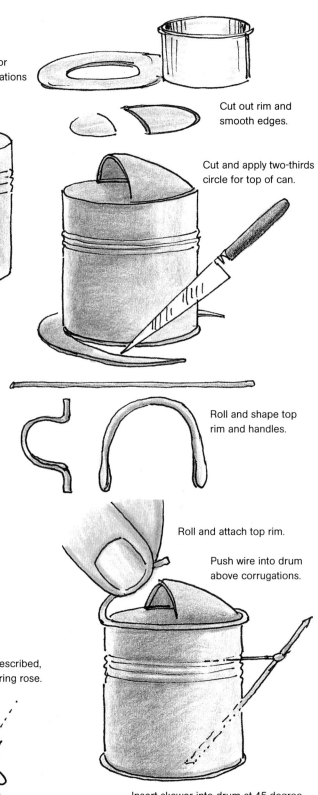

Cut out rim and smooth edges.

Cut and apply two-thirds circle for top of can.

Roll and shape top rim and handles.

Roll and attach top rim.

Push wire into drum above corrugations.

Insert skewer into drum at 45 degree angle, and glue to wire.

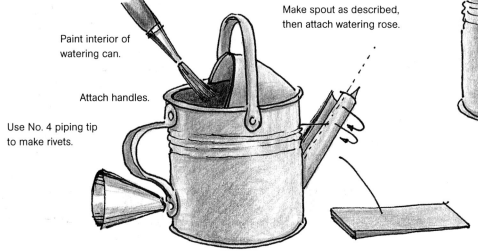

Paint interior of watering can.

Make spout as described, then attach watering rose.

Attach handles.

Use No. 4 piping tip to make rivets.

Make watering rose as described.

Brush watering can with lustre dust.

Make rabbit's ears and insert into can.

Paint brown wash on creases and joins.

RABBIT'S EARS

Roll light brown icing thinly and cut two pointy ear shapes. Cut two slightly smaller inner ear shapes from thinly rolled pink icing. Adhere the inner ears to the outer ears with a dab of water, then insert a support wire into the bottom of each ear and smooth and mould the ears with your fingers. Gently push the support wires into the watering can, adding a dab of water where the ears meet the cylinder.

GARDENING GLOVES

Roll light grey icing to 3 mm (1/8 in) thick and, with a sharp knife, cut out two glove shapes. Indent wristband by pressing with the frilling tool and push the tool into the end of each glove to create the idea of an opening. Push the back of a knife into the icing to mark the 'leather' sections of the gloves and use a tracing wheel or frilling tool to mark the stitching. Mix colour paste of your choice with alcohol and paint the details on the gloves, as pictured, including white-white colour paste stitching.

Assembling cakes

Allow some dark brown icing to dry, then crumble or chop into 'soil'. Attach this 'soil' to the top of the brown-covered cupcake with a little water, leaving a hole for the carrot. Airbrush the top of the cake with lighter brown colour. Insert the carrot into the hole with a dab of water. Attach the other models to their relevant cakes with a dab of water.

Chop dry brown icing onto top of cupcake, leaving hole for carrot.

Airbrush with brown wash.

Insert carrot.

PAINTING

Mix black colour paste with alcohol and paint the 'interior' of the can dark, at the top. For a rust effect, mix brown colour paste with alcohol and paint along joins, rims, rivets and corrugations. Mix silver lustre dust with alcohol and paint the lighter, more used, 'exposed' areas of the watering can to give a shiny effect.

Cut glove shape from light grey icing.

Indent with back of knife.

Mark details with frilling tool.

Mark stitch marks with a tracing wheel.

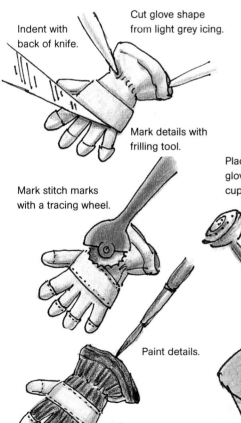

Paint details.

Place can and gloves on green cupcake.

Place rest of vegetables on marble-effect bases.

Dinosaur eggs

I had breakfast with my six-year-old godson Charlie who told me earnestly to be very careful when tapping my boiled egg as there could be a baby dinosaur inside. The best thing about being a cake decorator is that we can make dreams come true; this design is also a great introduction to figurine modelling.

Materials

6 cupcakes
300 g (10$\frac{1}{2}$ oz) ganache
100 ml (3$\frac{1}{2}$ fl oz) syrup
Cornflour in shaker
Approximately 1 kg (2 lb 4 oz) fondant icing
Colour paste: green, blue, orange, yellow, black, purple, brown, white-white
Airbrush colour: purple, blue, red, green
Cake-decorating alcohol
Royal icing
Tylose powder
Piping gel
White lustre powder

Equipment

Large and small rolling pins
Cranked palette knife
Small sharp kitchen knife
Scissors
Flexi-smoother
Pastry brush
Frilling tool
Fine and medium paintbrushes
Piping bag
No. 2 piping tip
Circle cutters
Airbrush machine
Bamboo skewers
50 cm (20 in) square cake board (optional)

Techniques checklist

Recipes (page 204)
Colouring fondant icing (page 210)
Red and black icing (page 211)
Covering cupcakes (page 209)
Figurine modelling (page 218)
Airbrushing (page 216)
Edible painting and colour wash (page 213)
Gelling (page 213)
Eyes (page 215)

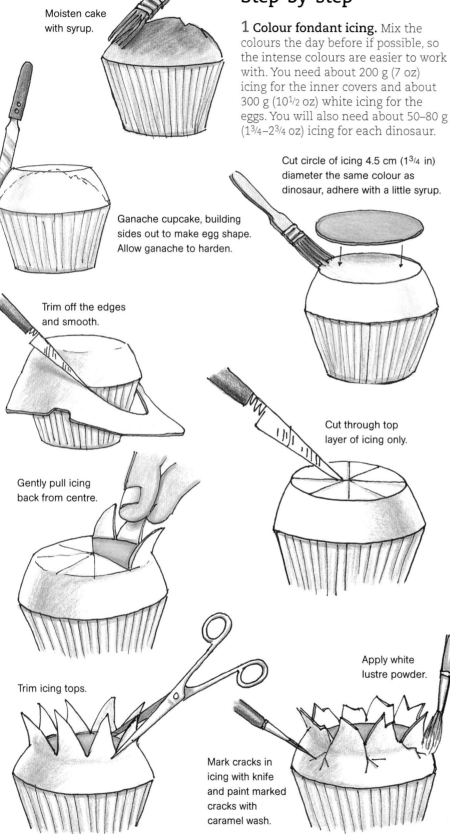

Moisten cake with syrup.

Ganache cupcake, building sides out to make egg shape. Allow ganache to harden.

Trim off the edges and smooth.

Gently pull icing back from centre.

Trim icing tops.

Cut through top layer of icing only.

Cut circle of icing 4.5 cm (1¾ in) diameter the same colour as dinosaur, adhere with a little syrup.

Mark cracks in icing with knife and paint marked cracks with caramel wash.

Apply white lustre powder.

Step-by-step

1 Colour fondant icing. Mix the colours the day before if possible, so the intense colours are easier to work with. You need about 200 g (7 oz) icing for the inner covers and about 300 g (10½ oz) white icing for the eggs. You will also need about 50–80 g (1¾–2¾ oz) icing for each dinosaur.

2 Ganache cupcakes. For these cupcakes, the method of ganaching is slightly different to the usual, because you need to build up a base for the egg. Brush the cupcakes with syrup and ganache the cakes, building the sides out to make the egg shape, as shown. Flatten the top to 4.5 cm (1¾ in) in diameter and leave the ganache to harden.

3 Add inner covers. Roll out icing (the same colours you will use for the dinosaurs) to about 3 mm (⅛ in) thick and, using a round 4.5 cm (1¾ in) cutter, cut a disc. Brush the top of the cake with syrup and adhere the cover to the cake.

4 Make eggshells. Knead some Tylose into the white icing, roll out to 3 mm (⅛ in) thick and cut a circle, about 10–12 cm (4–5 in) in diameter. Apply syrup to the ganached sides of the cake only, making sure to avoid the fondant-covered top. Cover cake with the circle of icing, smooth in place with a flexi-smoother and trim away excess icing. Once the cupcakes are covered, take a small clean knife and, with great care, cut through the top layer of icing only, making four shallow cuts across the top of each cake — vertical, horizontal and along each diagonal. This will divide the top of the cake into eight segments. Very gently peel back the segments from the centre, like a flower, exposing the coloured icing underneath.

Using scissors, trim the tips of the segments so that they are less regular and more like a cracked egg. Mark cracks in the eggshell with a sharp knife or frilling tool.

Mix brown colour paste with alcohol to a caramel colour and paint the cracks in the eggshell. Allow to dry, then brush white lustre powder over the surface of the eggshell with a dry paintbrush.

5 Make dinosaurs.

Planetosaurus

Our Planetosaurus dinosaurs are variations on the brontosaurus (apatosaurus) and stegosaurus. Follow our designs or create your own fantastical creatures. When choosing colours, let your imagination be your guide — and add colour and spots wherever you fancy! Spines, horns and teeth can be piped on or rolled and cut from fondant icing. As these little dinosaurs are just hatching from their eggs, their teeth and horns are quite small — if you decide to make larger ones, for extra fierceness, you might need to add skewers in places, to help support the weight.

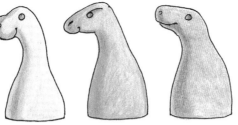

Make base colours and roll out three dinosaur shapes.

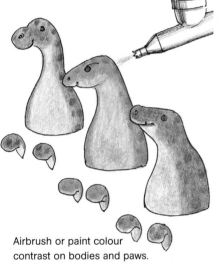

Roll out and shape paws.

Shape nose.

Mark eyes, nostrils and mouth.

Make sure there is enough space for body to fit snugly within eggshell and insert gelled skewer.

Airbrush or paint colour contrast on bodies and paws.

FINISHING Roll small balls of black icing and adhere to the eye sockets with a dab of water. Paint the eyes with piping gel and, when completely dry, add white-white colour paste highlights. Mix black colour paste with alcohol and, using a fine paintbrush, paint in the mouth and nostrils. Add a dab of water to the base of the dinosaur and gently lower it into position inside the eggshell. Position the paws in place with a dab of water. Using white royal icing and a No. 2 piping tip, pipe the claws onto the paws. Alternatively, roll and flatten tiny claws from white fondant and apply with a dab of water.

AIRBRUSHING Fill the reservoir on the airbrush with alcohol and a little airbrush colour and spray each dinosaur and paws with a darker colour than the base colour, leaving the base colour untouched on the undersides of the paws and on the chin and chest areas. Spray or paint spots in a contrasting colour, if desired. Leave to dry.

Insert dinosaur into eggshell.

Roll out black balls for eyes.

Add feet and pipe claws.

HEAD, BODY AND PAWS Knead a little Tylose powder into three golf ball-sized pieces of icing (we used blue, dark green and purple). Roll each ball into an elongated shape, as shown, approximately two-thirds body and one-third head. Flatten the base, making sure that the diameter of each lower body will fit snugly into its eggshell. Bend the necks to create heads with tapered or bulbous noses. Use a frilling tool to indent eye sockets, nostrils and mouths. Insert a gelled support skewer up the centre of each dinosaur from the base. Roll six pea-sized balls (two in each colour) for the paws and model into fat teardrop shapes, as shown.

SPINES For the purple dinosaur, roll out the white icing thinly and cut small rectangular-shaped spines. Attach each one with a dab of water. For the green dinosaur, pipe white spines down the back.

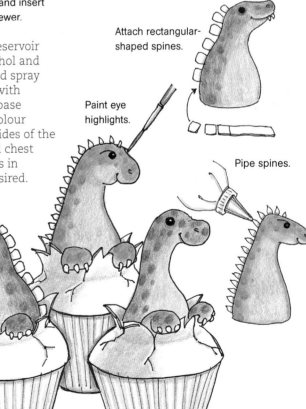

Attach rectangular-shaped spines.

Paint eye highlights.

Pipe spines.

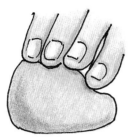

Roll out and shape
triceratops base colour.

Cut in half, and shape body.
Insert support skewer.

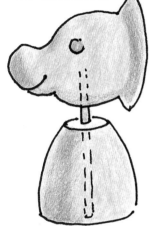

Triceratops

HEAD AND BODY Knead a little
Tylose powder into a small golf
ball-sized piece of icing in the colour
of your choice (we used yellow as a
base colour). Roll the icing into a ball
and cut in half. Shape one half into
a fat egg with a flat bottom for the
body, making sure that the diameter
of the lower body will fit snugly into
the eggshell. Insert a gelled skewer
support into the body, leaving a short
length extending at the top for
inserting into the head. Roll the other
half of the icing into a cone shape,

tapering and rounding it at the nose
end, as shown. Gently press with your
fingers to define the nose and mark
the jawline with a frilling tool. Pinch
the icing around the back of the head
to form the skull plate. Use scissors
to trim off any excess or uneven icing
and smooth to an edge with your
fingers. Indent the eye sockets, mouth
and nostrils with a frilling tool. Make
paws as for the Planetosaurus. Add
a dab of water to the underside of the
head and carefully lower it onto the
extending skewer on the body.

Trim off excess.

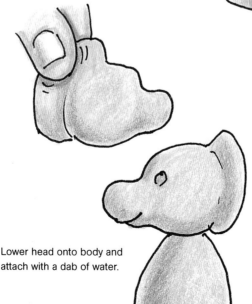

Mark eyes, nostrils and
mouth indentation.

Pinch icing at back of
head to form skull plate.

Airbrush body and paws
leaving base colour on
underside of paws, chin
and chest.

Shape head, mark jawline
and mould nose.

Make paws.

Lower head onto body and
attach with a dab of water.

AIRBRUSHING Fill the reservoir
on the airbrush with a little alcohol
and a little airbrush colour and spray
the dinosaur and paws or arms with
a contrast colour to the base colour,
leaving the base colour showing
on the undersides of the paws
and on the chin and chest areas.
If desired, dilute brown colour paste
with alcohol and paint faint spots
on the head area and skull plate.
Leave to dry.

Tyrannosaurus rex

HEAD AND BODY Knead a little Tylose powder into two golf ball-sized pieces of icing (we used yellow). Roll the icing into the shape of fat pears with the top of each pear lengthened for the neck, then folded over and squared off for the head. Use your fingers or a frilling tool to make an indent in the head, between the eyes. Using the photograph on page 153 as a guide, make indents for the eye sockets, mouths and nostrils with a frilling tool. Flatten the base, making sure the diameter of the lower body will fit snugly into the eggshell.

Bend arms at elbow, then attach to body.

Pipe on horns and teeth with No 2 piping tip.

Paint mouth and nostril details.

Airbrush or paint colour and spot contrasts, if desired, on body and feet.

FINISHING Roll small balls of black icing and adhere to the eye sockets with a dab of water. Paint the eyes with piping gel to make them shiny and, when completely dry, add white-white colour paste highlights. Mix black colour paste with alcohol and, using a fine paintbrush, paint in the mouth and nostrils. For the green dinosaur and the triceratops, position the paws in place on the front of the body with a dab of water. Add a dab of water to the base of each dinosaur and gently lower it into position inside its eggshell. Using white royal icing and a No. 2 piping tip, pipe on nose, skull plate horns and teeth, as shown. Pipe claws onto the paws. Alternatively, roll and flatten tiny horns and claws from white fondant and apply with a dab of water.

PAWS Note that only one of these Tyrannosaurus rex dinosaurs has arms (the other is just emerging from its egg). Roll two sausages of icing (we used green) and slightly flatten one end of each a little with your finger for adhering the arm to the body. Flatten the other end of each sausage and use a small sharp knife to trim into claws. Round the edges a little with your finger. Bend the arms at the elbow. Attach the arms to the body with a dab of water. Leave to dry, then airbrush and paint.

Roll out black balls for eyes.

Make sure bodies can fit within eggs.

Place finished dinosaurs into eggs.

Paint eye details and highlights.

Roll out arms and flatten ends.

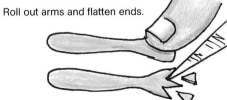

Cut claws with a sharp knife.

Pipe claws with No 2 piping tip.

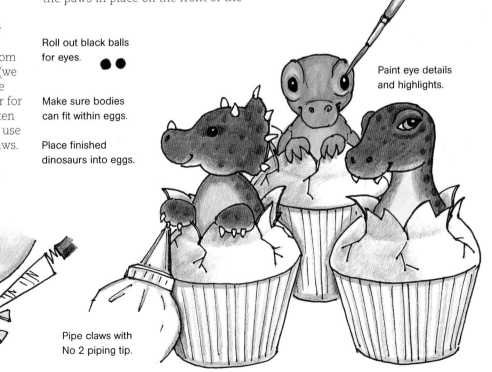

Cupcakes in a hurry

These dudes are as cool as it gets in the cupcake world; they have so much character they actually remind me of people I know. This story also introduces the design concept of using the whole cupcake rather than just the top, which creates a unique and amusing effect.

Materials

5 ganached cupcakes
100 ml (3½ fl oz) syrup
Cornflour in shaker
1.4 kg (3 lb 2 oz) fondant icing
Colour paste: green, brown, black, blue, red, yellow, orange, white-white
Tylose powder
Cake-decorating alcohol
Royal icing
Edible silver lustre dust
Red and pink petal dust
Piping gel
Cotton wool, for exhaust

Equipment

Large and small rolling pins
Cranked palette knife
Small sharp kitchen knife
Flexi-smoother
Pastry brush
Frilling tool
Balling tool
Fine and medium paintbrushes
Circle cutters
Dried spaghetti, toothpicks and thin bamboo skewers
Glue gun
50 cm (20 in) square cake board (optional)

Techniques checklist

Recipes (page 204)
Ganaching cupcakes (page 208)
Colouring fondant icing (page 210)
Red and black icing (page 211)
Covering cupcakes (page 209)
Figurine modelling (page 218)
Eyes (page 215)
Gelling (page 213)
Blush (page 214)
Edible painting and colour wash (page 213)

Step-by-step

Ganache cupcake.

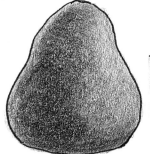

Shape icing to make a soft conical shape for head.

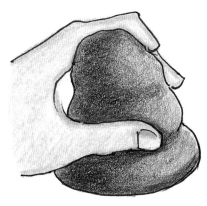

Use fingers and frilling tool to create creases, starting from the base and working upwards.

1 Colour fondant icing. Mix colours the day before if possible, to make intense colours easier to work with. The ganached cakes are not covered with fondant icing before decorating, so you do not need to allow for covers. However, you will require up to 230 g (8 oz) icing per cupcake for the figurines in brown (x 2), pale blue, green and white, as well as small amounts of red, blue, dark brown, light brown, black, bright green, white, orange and yellow, for the details.

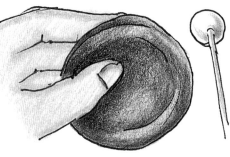

Use thumbs and balling tool to make indent to fit over cupcake.

Use cutter to trim any excess, then smooth edges.

2 Make the figurines.

Note Before making each of the following models and details, knead a little Tylose powder into the icing for extra hardness.

Heads

The heads are all begun in the same basic way, then varied according to the individual character. Follow the instructions for the basic head shape, then see individual details. Make and decorate one figurine at a time, so you can work while the icing is still soft. Mould icing into a soft conical shape. We used about 190 g (6¾ oz) for the racing driver, 200 g (7 oz) for the cyclist and 230 g (8 oz) each for the scuba diver, pilot and skier. Use your thumbs and a balling tool to create an indent in the bottom of the cone to fit perfectly over the dome of the cupcake. Use your fingers and a frilling tool to create creases in the body, starting at the bottom and working up to the top, using the diagrams for each character as a guide. Use a 7 cm (2¾ in) round cutter to trim off any excess icing around the lower edge. Attach the head to the ganached cupcake with some piping gel or syrup. Trim excess icing at the top of the figurine with a knife or scissors. Smooth with your fingers. Roll and attach a nose and use a frilling tool to indent the individual facial features, as shown in the diagrams.

Trim excess from top.

Smooth top and use frilling tool to indent facial features. Roll and attach nose to face.

Racing driver

WHEELS Roll black icing to 3 mm (¹⁄₈ in) thick and cut two 3 cm (1¹⁄₄ in) diameter circles. Stretch the edges a little into slight oval shapes. Cut two smaller circles from yellow icing, thread a black and yellow circle onto two spaghetti skewers and finish each with a small black icing 'hubcap'. Skewer a wheel into each side of the cupcake, through the paper case. (Use a toothpick or skewer to make a small hole in the paper case first, if necessary.)

GOGGLES Roll out black icing thinly and cut a narrow strip, long enough and wide enough for the goggles. Remove a 3 cm (1¹⁄₄ in) long rectangle from the centre of the strip, as shown, and insert an identical piece, cut from white icing. Mix black colour paste with alcohol and paint eyes, leaving a tiny wedge of white in each circle as a highlight. Thin the paint and shade the top of the goggles with a grey colour wash. Allow paint to dry, then paint white area with piping gel. Add a fine yellow strip of trim to sides of goggles, then fix them in place on the face with a dab of water.

FINISHING Roll a tiny ball of red icing, flatten into a tongue shape and attach it to the mouth. Rub petal dust into cheeks with a dry paintbrush. Glue cotton wool around the end of a skewer and insert the stick into the back of the cupcake for exhaust smoke. Rotate each wheel on a slight angle to give the appearance of speed.

Attach cotton wool to skewer and insert into cupcake for exhaust fumes.

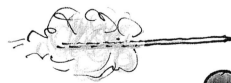

Make tongue and attach to mouth.

Cut circles for wheels, stretch ends a little.

Insert spaghetti through cupcake, attach wheel, yellow trim and hubcap.

HELMET Roll white icing to 3 mm (¹⁄₈ in) thick and use a 7 cm (2³⁄₄ in) round cutter to cut two overlapping circles, as shown. Remove the centre piece and use this piece to shape into a helmet. Cut a small visor for front of helmet and adhere both to the top of the figurine with a dab of water.

Cut two overlapping circles, remove centre piece and use to shape helmet.

For goggles, roll out black icing, cut out centre rectangle and insert white. Paint on eyes.

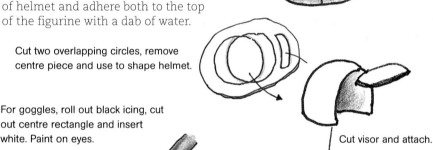

Paint eyes, leaving a tiny wedge of white. Shade goggles with grey colour wash. When dry, paint white area with piping gel and add yellow strips. Attach to face.

Racing driver (side view).

Racing driver (front view).

Cut visor and attach.

Attach helmet to top of head and add yellow trim. Rub petal dust into cheeks.

Angle wheels to give impression of speed.

Cyclist
(side view).

Cyclist
(front view).

Cyclist

HELMET Using the illustrations as a guide, shape a bike helmet from black icing and indent grooves with a frilling tool. Roll out green icing very thinly and smooth it over the helmet, gently pressing the icing into the grooves. Use a small sharp knife to cut away the green icing from the ends of the grooves, as shown, exposing the black underneath. Add a fine orange stripe trim, if desired. Fix helmet to head with a dab of water. Cut tiny straps from brown icing, mark with a frilling tool and fix to the sides of the head.

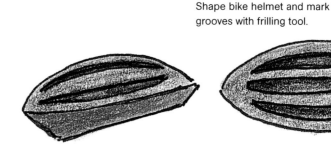

Shape bike helmet and mark grooves with frilling tool.

Cover with green icing and press it into grooves.

Cut away green icing at ends of grooves to reveal black.

Add orange trim if desired.

WHEELS Construct two wheels, as for racing driver, making outer wheels from blue icing, and adding white hubcaps. Mix black colour paste with alcohol and paint the spokes of the wheels with a fine paintbrush. Using spaghetti skewers, insert the wheels into the sides of the cupcake, on an angle to indicate speed.

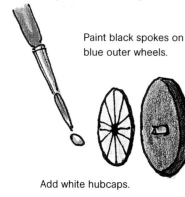

Paint black spokes on blue outer wheels.

Add white hubcaps.

FINISHING Roll two small white eyes to fit eye sockets, fix in place, then paint in a green iris and black pupil and finish with piping gel. When dry, add two tiny white-white colour paste highlights. Roll thin white icing and cut to fit mouth indent. Mark teeth with a frilling tool and attach to mouth with a dab of water. Rub a little red and pink petal dust into the cheeks.

Add blush.

Construct wheels as for racing driver and attach to cupcake, angled to show speed, with spaghetti skewers.

Shape eyes, attach and paint. Add gel, allow to dry then add highlights.

Cut out and mark teeth, and insert in mouth.

Attach helmet strap.

Scuba diver

FLIPPERS Roll out green icing and cut flipper shapes 5 cm (2 in) long, tapering in a wedge from thickest part at heel to thinner at toe end, as shown. Smooth and bend flippers to shape, and insert a gelled support skewer into each. Allow to dry before inserting skewers into the back of the cupcake, through the paper case.

SNORKEL Insert a toothpick into a sausage of green icing and roll it until it is as thin as you need. Leaving the toothpick embedded in the straight section of snorkel, cut the tube to size allowing a little extra at one end, to be curved around. Attach a small, oval-shaped piece of black icing to mouth for a mouthpiece, then attach snorkel to head and attach the end of the curved section to the mouthpiece.

GOGGLES Roll out white icing to 1 cm (½ in) thick and cut out the shape of the goggles glass, as shown. Roll and cut a very thin 1 cm (½ in) wide strip of green icing and adhere around edge of goggles, cutting and smoothing edges flush together. Mix black colour paste with alcohol and paint eyes, as for racing driver. Paint the 'glass' with piping gel when dry. Adhere goggles to face with a dab of water. Roll and cut a thin black strip for the goggles strap and attach it to sides of goggles and around the head, taking it over the snorkel, as shown.

Flipper (top view).

Flipper (side view).

Roll out tapered icing and cut shape. Smooth and bend, insert skewer and allow to dry.

Scuba diver shape (side view).

Scuba diver shape (front view).

Roll out and cut goggles glass.

Roll out a thin strip of green icing and wrap it around goggles.

For the snorkel, insert toothpick in straight section, roll to cover evenly, then bend end.

Paint on eyes.

Add blush.

Make mouthpiece and adhere to face.

Attach snorkel to head, bend and attach to mouthpiece.

Attach flippers.

Gel goggles.

FINISHING Rub petal dust into cheeks with a dry paintbrush, and attach flippers.

Pilot shape
(side view).

Pilot shape
(front view).

Pilot

HELMET Roll out light brown icing to 3 mm (⅛ in) thick and cut out helmet shape, as shown. Mark centre stitching line with a frilling tool and adhere helmet to head with a dab of water.

GOGGLES From thinly rolled dark brown icing cut a narrow strap to fit around the head and adhere in place. Roll two pea-sized balls of brown icing, squash to 6 mm (¼ in) thick and indent eye area. Roll and insert two tiny balls of white icing and smooth. Adhere goggles to face and smooth join. Mix black colour paste with alcohol and paint pupils as for Racing driver. Add piping gel when dry.

SCARF From thinly rolled red icing, cut two strips for a scarf, one to fit around 'neck' of cake, and the second bent in half for the scarf ends. Roll and flatten a small ball for the knot. Fray the ends of the scarf with a knife. Adhere the scarf around the neck and add the scarf ends and the knot.

PROPELLER Roll red icing to 3 mm (⅛ in) thick and cut a 3 cm-diameter (1¼ in) circle. Remove a 2.5cm (1 in) diameter circle from the centre and replace with an identical circle cut from blue icing. (Remember to adhere the edges.) Skewer the propeller on a length of spaghetti and cover the end with a knob of red icing.

Cut out pilot's helmet shape.

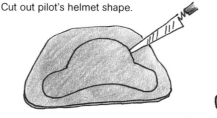

Make goggle strap and adhere to head.

Make propeller as described.

Skewer with spaghetti.

Attach propeller and paint spinning lines.

WINGS AND FUSELAGE Model wings and sections of fuselage from red icing, as shown, inserting a length of spaghetti into each piece. Join tail fins to tail of fuselage with a dab of water. Paint the pieces of plane with piping gel to make them shiny.

Make goggles, indent eye area, insert white eye, smooth, paint and gel. Attach to face.

Add blush.

Make aeroplane parts as described, insert skewers, and paint with gel.

Make scarf band and adhere around neck.

Make scarf ends and knot, and attach.

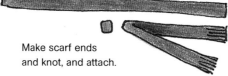

FINISHING Insert propeller, wings and fuselage into the cupcake at appropriate points. Mix black colour paste with alcohol and paint fine concentric circles on the propeller to indicate speed. Rub a little petal dust into the cheeks.

Skier

TEETH While the icing is still soft, indent and shape the skier's mouth with a frilling tool and mark the teeth with a sharp knife.

GOGGLES Make as for scuba diver, using blue icing to outline the 'glass'.

BEANIE Roll yellow icing to 3 mm (^{1}/8 in) thick and cut a 5 cm (2 in) diameter circle. Remove a 3.5 cm (1^3/8 in) diameter circle from the centre and replace with an identical circle cut from blue icing. Remove a 2.5 cm (1 in) circle from the centre of the blue circle and replace it with an identical circle in yellow. (Remember to adhere all the edges.) Cut the finished circle in half, discard one half and wrap the remaining half around the head, smoothing the edges together at the back. Roll a thin strip of blue icing, mark into a ribbed band and adhere to lower edge of beanie. Roll and attach a tiny blue ball for a pompom.

SKIS AND POLES Roll out yellow icing to 3 mm (^{1}/8 in) thick and cut two ski shapes, as shown. Turn up the pointy ends and support them until dry. For the poles, trim two skewers to 8 cm (3^1/4 in) long and trim another two to 4 cm (1^1/2 in) long for the support sticks. Glue-gun the support sticks at right angles to the poles, as shown, about 2 cm (^{3}/4 in) from the ends. Mix a little silver dust and alcohol, paint the poles and allow to dry. Make handles and circular ends of poles from black icing and adhere in position. Cut mitten shapes from blue icing and fold the mittens around the poles, covering the join between the pole and support stick.

Cut out ski shapes and turn up pointy ends. Support with icing until dry.

Glue-gun support stick to ski pole.

Paint poles silver.

Make handles and round ends for poles.

Cut mitten shapes and fold mittens around poles.

Make goggles as for scuba diver, but with blue rim.

Make beanie from matching circles. Cut in half and discard half.

Wrap beanie around head. Add blue band and mark with frilling tool.

SCARF Roll and adhere strips of blue and yellow icing together, then trim horizontally into a striped scarf. Cut two scarf ends (fray the ends with a knife) and a knot, then assemble all the pieces around the 'neck' of the skier.

FINISHING Push the support sticks of the poles into the sides of the cupcake and set the finished cake on top of the skis. Add petal dust blush to cheeks, nose and chin.

Join strips of colour and trim to make scarf pieces.

Attach scarf pieces around neck.

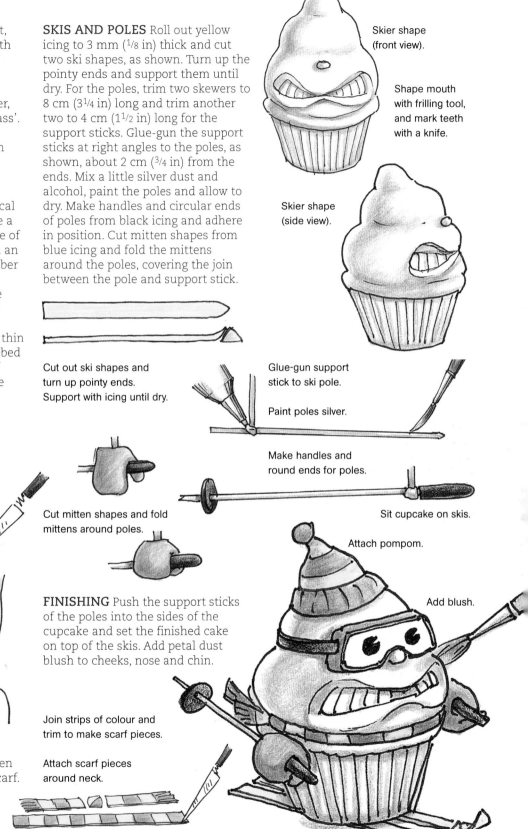

Skier shape (front view).

Shape mouth with frilling tool, and mark teeth with a knife.

Skier shape (side view).

Sit cupcake on skis.

Attach pompom.

Add blush.

Fairy tea party

You cannot have a cupcake book without a fairy tea party; after all, cupcakes are often called fairy cakes. This story introduces a realistic fairy figurine who looks like my daughter, Estelle. Figurine making is easier if you have an artistic bent or training, but the story works just as well without the figurine, as the recipients themselves could be fairies!

Materials

6 ganached cupcakes
100 ml (3½ fl oz) syrup
Cornflour in shaker
750 g (1 lb 10 oz) fondant icing
Colour paste: green, pink, blue,
    red, brown, caramel, yellow,
    white-white
Cake-decorating alcohol
Airbrush colour: dark green
    (optional)
Royal icing
Edible gold lustre dust
Red and pink petal dust
Tylose powder
Piping gel

Equipment

Large and small rolling pins
Cranked palette knife
Small sharp kitchen knife
Flexi-smoother
Pastry brush
Frilling tool
Fine and medium paintbrushes
Piping bags
No. 2 and No. 3 piping tips
Star tip
Circle cutters
Flower cutter (6 cm/2½ in)
Teacup and saucer mould
    (see page 220)
5 cm (2 in) diameter
    polystyrene ball
Glue gun
22-gauge florist's wire
Toothpicks and thin bamboo
    skewers or dried spaghetti,
    for support
Synthetic scourer
Airbrush machine (optional)
2–4 decorative butterflies
    (from craft shops)
50 cm (20 in) square cake board
    (optional)

Techniques checklist

Recipes (page 204)
Ganaching cupcakes (page 208)
Colouring fondant icing
    (page 210)
Red and black icing (page 211)
Skin-coloured icing (page 211)
Covering cupcakes (page 209)
Figurine modelling (page 218)
Making simple moulds
    (page 220)
Airbrushing (optional, page 216)
Eyes (page 215)
Gelling (page 213)
Blush (page 214)
Edible painting and colour wash
    (page 213)
Painting in silver or gold
    (page 214)

Step-by-step

1 Colour fondant icing. Mix the colours the day before if possible, to make the intense colours easier to work with. You will need about 500 g (1 lb 2 oz) white icing for the covers and models. You will also need about 100 g (3½ oz) each of green and pink icing for the flower shapes, about 30 g (1 oz) skin-coloured icing for the fairy, and small amounts of light green, blue, light caramel and dark brown.

2 Cover cupcakes. Allowing about 40 g (1½ oz) icing per cupcake, roll out white icing to 3 mm (⅛ in) thick and cover ganached cupcakes. Roll green and pink icing thinly and, using a 6 cm (2½ in) flower cutter (slightly smaller than the cover), cut three flowers in each colour and adhere to the tops of the covered cakes with a dab of water.

3 Make the decorations.

Note Before making each of the following models or figurines, knead a little Tylose powder into the icing for extra hardness.

Teapot

Glue-gun a wooden skewer into the centre of a 5 cm (2 in) diameter polystyrene ball. Roll about 50 g (1¾ oz) white icing out to 3 mm (⅛ in) thick. Paint the ball lightly with piping gel and drape the icing over the ball, smoothing it with your fingers. Trim the excess and smooth again. Press a 4.5 cm (1¾ in) round cutter lightly into the top of the ball to indent the lid. Make a spout and handle, as shown, indenting the spout with a frilling tool and inserting wires for support into each. Roll a pea-sized ball for the knob on the lid and insert a wire. Shape a round base, about 2.5 cm (1 in) in diameter and 6 mm (¼ in) high. Make a hole in the centre of the base so that it can be threaded onto the skewer. Applying a dab of water where surfaces will touch, push the wires on all components into teapot and thread base onto the skewer.

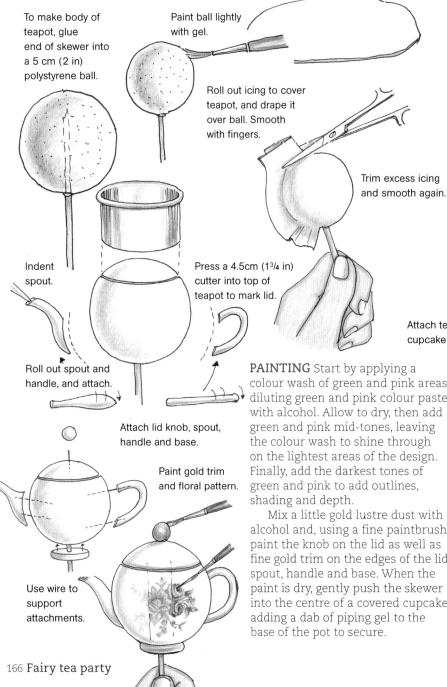

To make body of teapot, glue end of skewer into a 5 cm (2 in) polystyrene ball.

Paint ball lightly with gel.

Roll out icing to cover teapot, and drape it over ball. Smooth with fingers.

Trim excess icing and smooth again.

Indent spout.

Press a 4.5cm (1¾ in) cutter into top of teapot to mark lid.

Roll out spout and handle, and attach.

Attach lid knob, spout, handle and base.

Paint gold trim and floral pattern.

Use wire to support attachments.

Attach teapot to iced cupcake with skewer.

PAINTING Start by applying a colour wash of green and pink areas, diluting green and pink colour paste with alcohol. Allow to dry, then add green and pink mid-tones, leaving the colour wash to shine through on the lightest areas of the design. Finally, add the darkest tones of green and pink to add outlines, shading and depth.

Mix a little gold lustre dust with alcohol and, using a fine paintbrush, paint the knob on the lid as well as fine gold trim on the edges of the lid, spout, handle and base. When the paint is dry, gently push the skewer into the centre of a covered cupcake, adding a dab of piping gel to the base of the pot to secure.

Teacups

Glue a ping-pong ball onto a piece of wood. Roll out white icing to 3 mm (1/8 in) thick. Sprinkle with cornflour. Drape icing, cornflour side down, over the ball and trim excess at about the midpoint of the ball. Smooth with your fingers and allow to harden.

To make a base for the cup, roll out a pea-sized ball of icing to a disc about 1.8 cm (3/4 in) in diameter and adhere to the bottom of the cup with a dab of water. Use a skewer to make a hole through the centre of the base and cup. Invert mould and remove cup. Before the base has hardened, check that the cup is level, applying a little pressure to one side or the other if necessary, to even it up. For the handle, roll a thin sausage of white icing and bend it into shape, trimming the ends so it will fit exactly. Leave it to dry and harden.

For the contents of the cup, sprinkle the inside of a half ping-pong ball mould with cornflour, put a lump of icing into it and smooth to shape so it almost fills the mould. Allow to dry, remove from the mould and place it into the teacup with a dab of water. This makes a good base for whatever 'beverage' you wish to add to the cup.

Glue a whole ping-pong ball to a piece of wood to use as a mould.

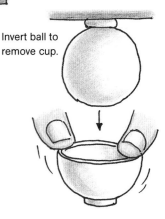

Roll out icing, sprinkle with cornflour and drape over ball. Trim, smooth and allow to harden.

Flatten a small ball of icing to make cup base and attach. Make hole in base with a skewer.

Invert ball to remove cup.

Glue half a ping-pong ball to a piece of wood. Sprinkle inside with cornflour, and press some icing into the ball to form a solid shape. When dry, remove and place in teacup.

Shape handle: use your cup as a guide for the handle position.

Saucers

Roll out and cut saucer and plate shapes.

Dust saucer mould with cornflour. Press and shape icing onto saucer mould.

Make centre hole in base with skewer.

Saucers

Roll out white icing to 3 mm (1/8 in) thick and cut out two 6 cm (2 1/4 in) circles. Dust the saucer mould (page 220) with cornflour. One at a time, push the icing onto the mould to shape saucer. Press a hole in the centre with a skewer. Allow to dry. Mix gold dust with alcohol and paint rims.

Assembling cups and saucers

Push a skewer through the bottom of the saucer and cup into the 'contents', then gel the extending stick and push it into the covered cupcake until it sits flush with the bottom of the cup, adding a dab of piping gel to the bottom of the saucer.

Attach the handle to the cup with two small dots of royal icing. Paint a design on the side of the cup as for the teapot, and finish the edges of the cup, saucers and plates with a fine gold rim.

To make 'tea', add a tiny amount of white-white colour paste to piping gel to make it opaque (but still shiny), then mix minute amounts of colour paste into the gel until it is the desired colour. Spoon the gel into the cup and smooth the surface with a palette knife.

Insert skewer through saucer into base of teacup and then secure to cupcake.

Adhere handle with royal icing.

Spoon 'tea' into cup and smooth with a palette knife.

Cakes and biscuits

PLATES Roll out white icing to 3 mm (¹/₈ in) thick and cut out two 7 cm (3 in) circles. Dust the saucer mould (used for making the saucers, page 167) with cornflour. One at a time, push the icing onto the mould to shape plate. Allow to dry. Mix gold dust with alcohol and paint the rims.

CAKE Roll a 3 cm (1¹/₄ in) diameter ball of light caramel icing into a wedge shape, as shown. Rough the sides and back edge with a synthetic scourer, to give a cake effect. Mix caramel colour paste with a little alcohol and paint the back edge of the wedge to make the cake look 'baked'. Cut the wedge in half horizontally. Thinly roll and cut a wedge of coloured icing for the cake and adhere to the top of one wedge with a dab of water. Pipe royal icing on top of the second wedge, using a star tip, and sandwich the two wedges together. Pipe small stars of royal icing along the back edge of the icing, to finish.

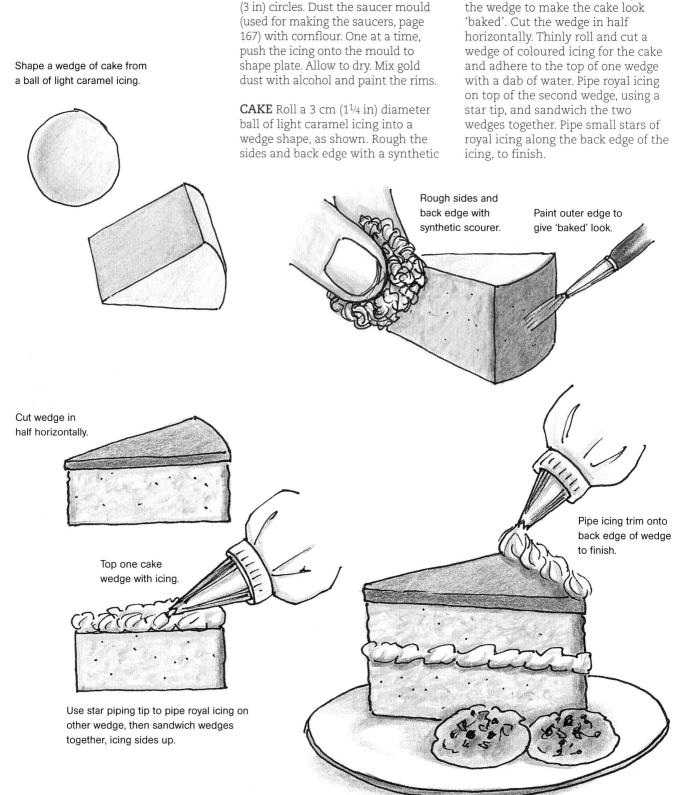

Shape a wedge of cake from a ball of light caramel icing.

Rough sides and back edge with synthetic scourer.

Paint outer edge to give 'baked' look.

Cut wedge in half horizontally.

Top one cake wedge with icing.

Use star piping tip to pipe royal icing on other wedge, then sandwich wedges together, icing sides up.

Pipe icing trim onto back edge of wedge to finish.

CUPCAKE Roll a 2 cm (¾ in) diameter ball of bright green icing and shape into the dome of a cupcake, as shown. If desired, mix a drop of green airbrush colour with alcohol and airbrush the outer edges of the dome. Take a 2 cm (¾ in) diameter ball of white icing and shape into a cone for the base of the cupcake. Mark the paper case lines with a knife. Mix brown colour paste and alcohol to a caramel colour and paint the paper case. Attach the dome of the cupcake to the paper case with a dab of water.

CHOC-CHIP BISCUITS Allow a small amount of dark brown icing to dry out and crumble or chop it into tiny pieces for choc chips. Press pea-sized balls of light ochre icing to 6 mm (¼ in) rounds and rough the surface with a synthetic scourer, as for the cake. Dab the surface with water and attach the choc chips. Paint the top of the biscuits with a caramel wash, as before, to make them look baked.

Shape top of cupcake.

Airbrush around edge (optional).

Shape cupcake base.

Mark with knife to make paper case.

Paint paper case and assemble cupcake.

ASSEMBLE BAKED GOODS
Position the cakes and biscuits onto the gold-rimmed plates with a dab of water and add a paper butterfly to the top of the cupcake, if desired.

Chop or crumble some dry dark-brown icing for choc chips.

Decorate cupcake with butterfly, if desired.

Paint top of biscuit to give 'baked' look.

Press a small ball into a biscuit shape and rough up top with a synthetic scourer. Dab surface with water to attach choc chips.

Fairy

BASIC Roll a 2 cm (¾ in) diameter ball of skin-coloured icing and shape into an oval. Moisten the end of a skewer and insert it into the head from the bottom. Allow to dry, so the head is firmly held and not swivelling on the stick. Use a frilling tool to indent the eye area at about the halfway point on the face.

FACE Moisten the areas where you wish to build up the facial features — cheeks, forehead, back of head, nose, lips and chin — and roll and adhere small balls of icing to shape the face. You are going to cover these features with a second 'skin' so they will double in size — remember to allow for this when adding icing. Roll out skin-coloured icing to 2 mm (1/16 in) thick and drape it over the head base, smoothing it on gently to show the face contours underneath. Indent the eye area on either side of the nose, the area under the nose (to get a turned up effect) and around the sides of the mouth. Smooth the excess icing towards the back of the head, trim off excess and smooth with your fingers.

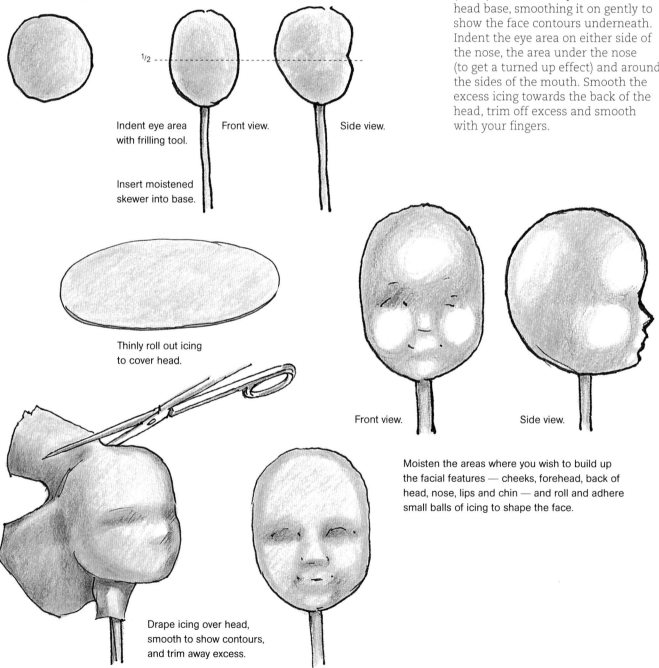

Roll out head shape.

Indent eye area with frilling tool.

Insert moistened skewer into base.

½

Front view.

Side view.

Thinly roll out icing to cover head.

Drape icing over head, smooth to show contours, and trim away excess.

Front view.

Side view.

Moisten the areas where you wish to build up the facial features — cheeks, forehead, back of head, nose, lips and chin — and roll and adhere small balls of icing to shape the face.

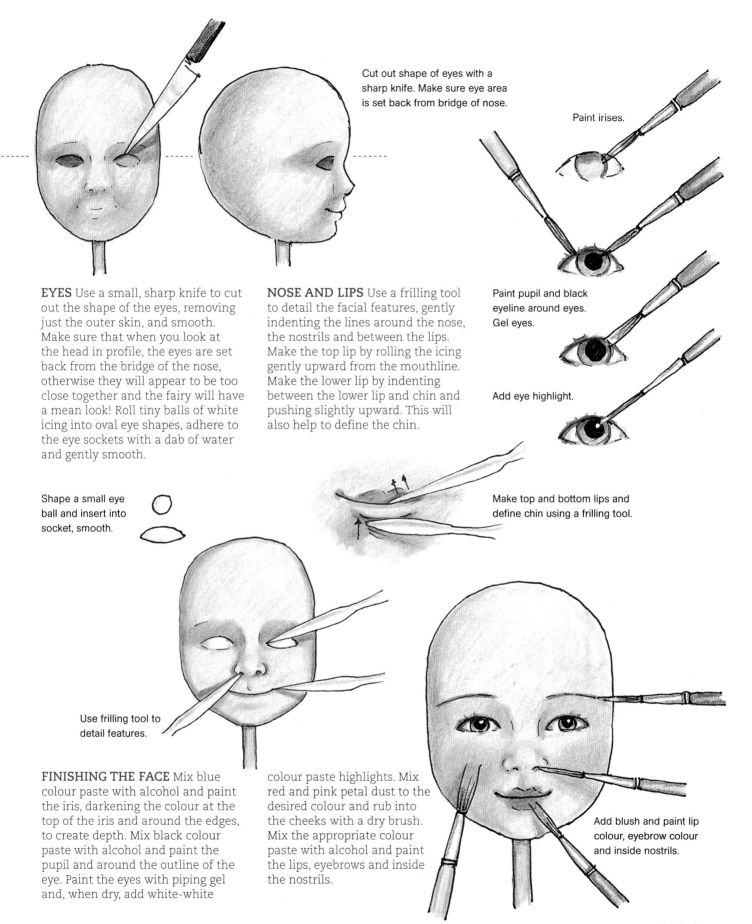

Cut out shape of eyes with a sharp knife. Make sure eye area is set back from bridge of nose.

Paint irises.

EYES Use a small, sharp knife to cut out the shape of the eyes, removing just the outer skin, and smooth. Make sure that when you look at the head in profile, the eyes are set back from the bridge of the nose, otherwise they will appear to be too close together and the fairy will have a mean look! Roll tiny balls of white icing into oval eye shapes, adhere to the eye sockets with a dab of water and gently smooth.

NOSE AND LIPS Use a frilling tool to detail the facial features, gently indenting the lines around the nose, the nostrils and between the lips. Make the top lip by rolling the icing gently upward from the mouthline. Make the lower lip by indenting between the lower lip and chin and pushing slightly upward. This will also help to define the chin.

Paint pupil and black eyeline around eyes. Gel eyes.

Add eye highlight.

Shape a small eye ball and insert into socket, smooth.

Make top and bottom lips and define chin using a frilling tool.

Use frilling tool to detail features.

FINISHING THE FACE Mix blue colour paste with alcohol and paint the iris, darkening the colour at the top of the iris and around the edges, to create depth. Mix black colour paste with alcohol and paint the pupil and around the outline of the eye. Paint the eyes with piping gel and, when dry, add white-white

colour paste highlights. Mix red and pink petal dust to the desired colour and rub into the cheeks with a dry brush. Mix the appropriate colour paste with alcohol and paint the lips, eyebrows and inside the nostrils.

Add blush and paint lip colour, eyebrow colour and inside nostrils.

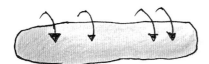

Roll out skin-coloured icing, tapering at the end where knees will be.

Fold body in half so that it is kneeling (side view).

BODY Roll about 20 g (¾ oz) skin-coloured icing to a fattish sausage, tapering it a little at one end where the knees will be. Fold the sausage into an L-shape, noting that the body should be about twice the height of the fairy's head. Gel the skewer extending from the head and gently insert it into the body, leaving a little of the stick exposed in the neck area. Roll a strip of skin-coloured icing and wrap it around the exposed stick, creating the neck. Trim off any excess and smooth. Lightly mark in contours of fairy's body, such as knees and lap, so that her dress will sit more naturally when you drape it over the body.

Roll out icing for dress.

Wrap icing around body, trim at back and smooth.

Gel skewer and insert head into body leaving a little skewer exposed.

Cover with a small strip of icing. Trim and smooth.

DRESS Roll out about 20 g (¾ oz) green icing and trim to a rectangle, about 7 cm x 8 cm (2¾ x 3¼ in) and 2 mm (¹⁄₁₆ in) thick. Wrap the icing around and under the fairy's body, trim away excess at the back and smooth with your fingers. Leave a little of the excess at the sides for the folds of the dress beneath her legs. Carefully cut out the neckline and armholes and smooth. Indent the bodice line and folds of the dress with a frilling tool.

Lightly mark body contours, especially legs.

Roll out icing for arms leaving slight bump in centre for hands.

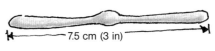

⊢ 7.5 cm (3 in) ⊣

Roll out strips for sleeves.

1 cm (½ in)

⊢ 3cm (1¼ in) ⊣

Gather sleeve to form pleats then attach to top of armholes.

Cut neckline and armholes with a knife. Smooth. Mark folds with a frilling tool.

Indent middle of hands for butterfly wire.

ARMS Roll out a single sausage of skin-coloured icing, as shown, shaping a slight bump in the middle for the hands. Using a dab of water, attach each end of the sausage to the armholes and make a hole in the middle of the hands for the butterfly wire. Roll out a 3 x 1 cm (1¼ x ½ in) strip of green icing for each sleeve. Gather one edge of each into small pleats. Attach sleeves to the top of the armholes with a dab of water.

HAIR Thinly roll out light brown icing and trim to a rectangle about 14 x 4 cm (5½ x 1½ in). Adding a dab of water where areas will touch, gather the rectangle into a loop around the fairy's head, as shown, and trim away excess icing at the top and back. Smooth the hair with your fingers and mark the hair into tresses with the frilling tool, snipping the bottom edges to bring some strands of hair onto the front of the shoulders. Mix brown or orange colour paste with alcohol and paint the hair in the desired colour.

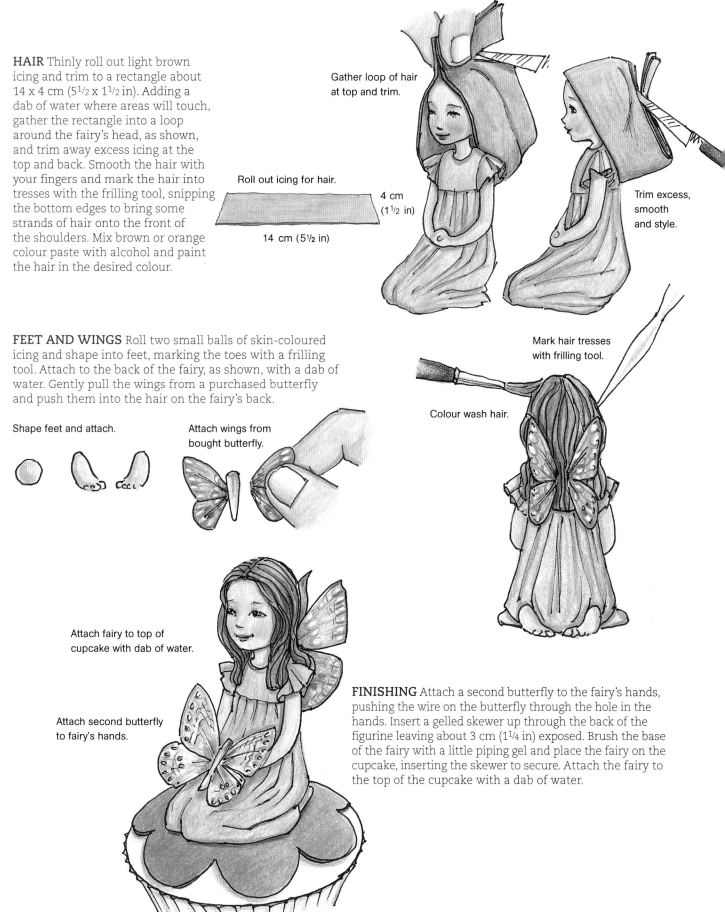

Roll out icing for hair.

14 cm (5½ in)

4 cm (1½ in)

Gather loop of hair at top and trim.

Trim excess, smooth and style.

FEET AND WINGS Roll two small balls of skin-coloured icing and shape into feet, marking the toes with a frilling tool. Attach to the back of the fairy, as shown, with a dab of water. Gently pull the wings from a purchased butterfly and push them into the hair on the fairy's back.

Shape feet and attach.

Attach wings from bought butterfly.

Mark hair tresses with frilling tool.

Colour wash hair.

Attach fairy to top of cupcake with dab of water.

Attach second butterfly to fairy's hands.

FINISHING Attach a second butterfly to the fairy's hands, pushing the wire on the butterfly through the hole in the hands. Insert a gelled skewer up through the back of the figurine leaving about 3 cm (1¼ in) exposed. Brush the base of the fairy with a little piping gel and place the fairy on the cupcake, inserting the skewer to secure. Attach the fairy to the top of the cupcake with a dab of water.

Save the planet

Most of the animals in this environmental story can be made from one piece of icing with legs, arms or wings (if applicable) to be added separately. Referring to toy or plastic animals or quality photographs will be a big help in achieving realistic results.

Materials

16 ganached cupcakes
160 ml (5¼ fl oz) syrup
Cornflour in shaker
Fondant icing
Tylose powder
Colour paste: green, olive green, blue, orange, yellow, pink, grey, brown, red, black, white-white
Airbrush colour: brown, green, blue
Cake-decorating alcohol
Royal icing
Piping gel

Equipment

Large and small rolling pins
Cranked palette knife
Small sharp kitchen knife
Flexi-smoother
Pastry brush
Frilling and balling tools
Fine and medium paintbrushes
Piping bag
No. 1, No. 2 and No. 3 piping tips
Circle cutters
Leaf-shaped cutter
Small sharp scissors
22-gauge florist's wire (or dried spaghetti)
Airbrush machine
Toothpicks and thin bamboo skewers
50 cm (20 in) square cake board (optional)

Techniques checklist

Recipes (page 204)
Ganaching cupcakes (page 208)
Colouring fondant icing (page 210)
Red and black icing (page 211)
Skin-coloured icing (page 211)
Covering cupcakes (page 209)
Figurine modelling (page 218)
Painting in silver or gold (page 214)
Edible painting and colour wash (page 213)
Eyes (page 215)
Marbling (page 212)
Gelling (page 213)

Polar bear

Beaver

Raccoon

Fawn

Panda

Koala

Cobra

Penguin

Llama

Giraffe

Fox

Tiger

Killer whale

Dolphin

Seal

Hippopotamus

Step-by-step

1 Colour the fondant icing. Mix the colours the day before if possible, to make the intense colours easier to work with.

2 Make decorations.

Note Before making each of the following models, knead a little Tylose powder into the icing for extra hardness. All these figurines can be made well in advance.

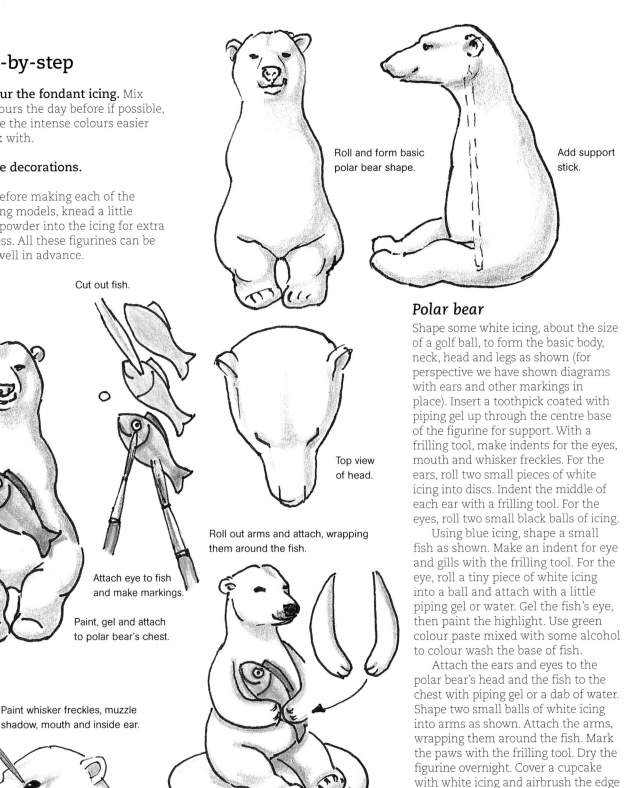

Cut out fish.

Roll and form basic polar bear shape.

Add support stick.

Attach eye to fish and make markings.

Paint, gel and attach to polar bear's chest.

Top view of head.

Roll out arms and attach, wrapping them around the fish.

Paint whisker freckles, muzzle shadow, mouth and inside ear.

Gel eyes and paint highlights.

Attach polar bear to cupcake.

Polar bear

Shape some white icing, about the size of a golf ball, to form the basic body, neck, head and legs as shown (for perspective we have shown diagrams with ears and other markings in place). Insert a toothpick coated with piping gel up through the centre base of the figurine for support. With a frilling tool, make indents for the eyes, mouth and whisker freckles. For the ears, roll two small pieces of white icing into discs. Indent the middle of each ear with a frilling tool. For the eyes, roll two small black balls of icing.

Using blue icing, shape a small fish as shown. Make an indent for eye and gills with the frilling tool. For the eye, roll a tiny piece of white icing into a ball and attach with a little piping gel or water. Gel the fish's eye, then paint the highlight. Use green colour paste mixed with some alcohol to colour wash the base of fish.

Attach the ears and eyes to the polar bear's head and the fish to the chest with piping gel or a dab of water. Shape two small balls of white icing into arms as shown. Attach the arms, wrapping them around the fish. Mark the paws with the frilling tool. Dry the figurine overnight. Cover a cupcake with white icing and airbrush the edge lightly with blue colour. Attach the figurine to the cupcake with piping gel. Gel the bear's eyes and paint white-white colour paste highlights. Paint nose, whisker freckles, shadow, mouth and inside-ear shadow with black colour paste mixed with alcohol.

Roll and form basic beaver shape. Insert support stick.

Make a criss-cross pattern on tail with frilling tool.

Top view of head.

Attach eyes and slightly yellowed teeth.

Beaver

Shape some light brown icing, the size of a golf ball, to form the basic body, neck, head and tail as shown (for perspective we have shown diagrams with ears and other markings in place). Make a criss-cross pattern on the tail with a frilling tool. Insert a toothpick coated with piping gel up through the centre of the figurine for extra support. Make indents for the eyes and an open mouth with the frilling tool. For the ears, roll two small pieces of light brown icing into balls and, using the end of the frilling tool, make an indent in the middle of each. Attach to the head with a dab of water.

For the arms and feet, shape small balls of light brown icing. Attach the arms (arrange so that he can hold a twig) and feet to the body with a dab of water or piping gel. Use a frilling tool to lightly mark the body, head and limbs to give the impression of fur. Airbrush the figurine using the photograph (see page 178) as a guide. Dry the figurine overnight.

For the eyes, roll two small black balls of icing. Take a rectangle of pale yellow icing and indent centre to mark two teeth. Attach the eyes and teeth with a dab of piping gel or water. Gel the eyes and paint the highlights. Cover a cupcake with pale olive-green icing and airbrush lightly around the edge with brown colour. Attach the figurine to the cupcake with piping gel. Paint nose and mouth with black colour paste mixed with alcohol. Place a twig in his hands.

Roll out arms and feet and mark fingers and toes with frilling tool.

Attach beaver's arms and arrange so they can hold a twig. Attach feet.

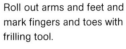

Airbrush shading onto beaver.

Gel eyes and paint nose and mouth.

Attach beaver to cupcake and place a twig in its arms.

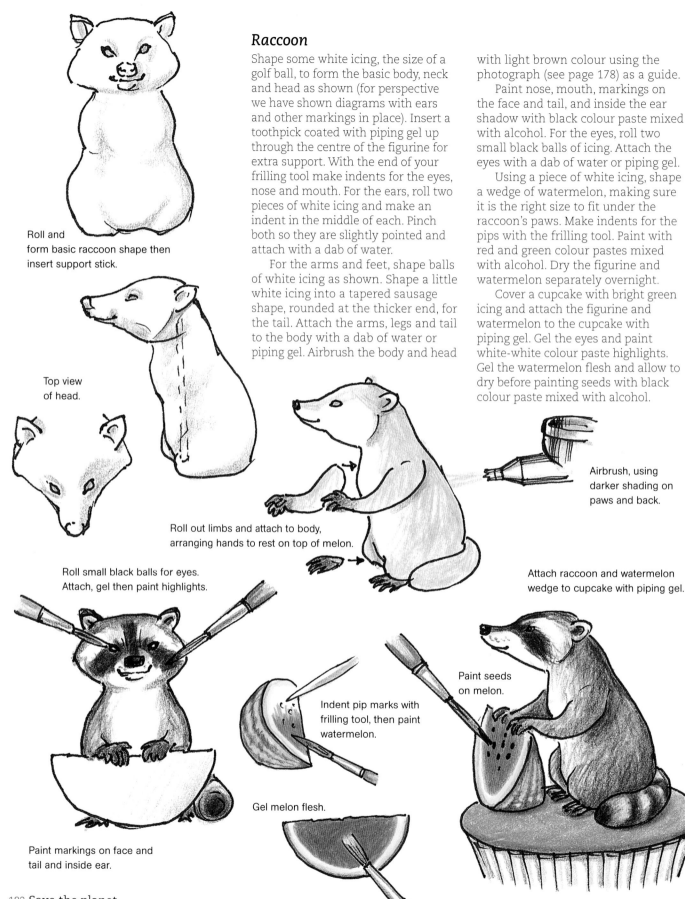

Raccoon

Shape some white icing, the size of a golf ball, to form the basic body, neck and head as shown (for perspective we have shown diagrams with ears and other markings in place). Insert a toothpick coated with piping gel up through the centre of the figurine for extra support. With the end of your frilling tool make indents for the eyes, nose and mouth. For the ears, roll two pieces of white icing and make an indent in the middle of each. Pinch both so they are slightly pointed and attach with a dab of water.

For the arms and feet, shape balls of white icing as shown. Shape a little white icing into a tapered sausage shape, rounded at the thicker end, for the tail. Attach the arms, legs and tail to the body with a dab of water or piping gel. Airbrush the body and head with light brown colour using the photograph (see page 178) as a guide.

Paint nose, mouth, markings on the face and tail, and inside the ear shadow with black colour paste mixed with alcohol. For the eyes, roll two small black balls of icing. Attach the eyes with a dab of water or piping gel.

Using a piece of white icing, shape a wedge of watermelon, making sure it is the right size to fit under the raccoon's paws. Make indents for the pips with the frilling tool. Paint with red and green colour pastes mixed with alcohol. Dry the figurine and watermelon separately overnight.

Cover a cupcake with bright green icing and attach the figurine and watermelon to the cupcake with piping gel. Gel the eyes and paint white-white colour paste highlights. Gel the watermelon flesh and allow to dry before painting seeds with black colour paste mixed with alcohol.

Roll and form basic raccoon shape then insert support stick.

Top view of head.

Roll out limbs and attach to body, arranging hands to rest on top of melon.

Airbrush, using darker shading on paws and back.

Roll small black balls for eyes. Attach, gel then paint highlights.

Attach raccoon and watermelon wedge to cupcake with piping gel.

Paint seeds on melon.

Indent pip marks with frilling tool, then paint watermelon.

Gel melon flesh.

Paint markings on face and tail and inside ear.

Fawn

Start with a piece of white icing about the size of a golf ball. Break off about two-thirds and shape it to form the basic body with front legs and neck as shown (for perspective we have shown diagrams with ears and other markings in place). Shape the remaining icing to form the head as shown. To attach the head to the body, brush a little piping gel over the top of the neck, insert a toothpick coated with piping gel, then place the head on top at desired angle. Make indents for the eyes, nose and mouth with a frilling tool. For the ears, roll two small pieces of white icing, then sculpt using your fingers and frilling tool. Insert a piece of spaghetti, leaving a little extending. Attach to the head with a dab of water.

For the back leg, shape a small ball of white icing as shown. Shape a little more white icing into a tail. Attach the leg and tail to the body with a dab of water or piping gel. Airbrush the fawn's body with brown or caramel colour using the photograph (see page 178) as a guide. Dry the figurine overnight.

For the eyes, shape two small black balls of icing. Paint the nose, muzzle, mouth line and hooves with black colour paste mixed with some alcohol.

To create the markings on the fawn's back, use a slightly moist fine paintbrush and lightly rub over small areas to remove the airbrush colour and expose the white underneath. Cover a cupcake in pale olive green and lightly airbrush the edge with brown colour if desired. Attach the figurine to the cupcake with piping gel. Gel eyes and paint white-white colour paste highlights.

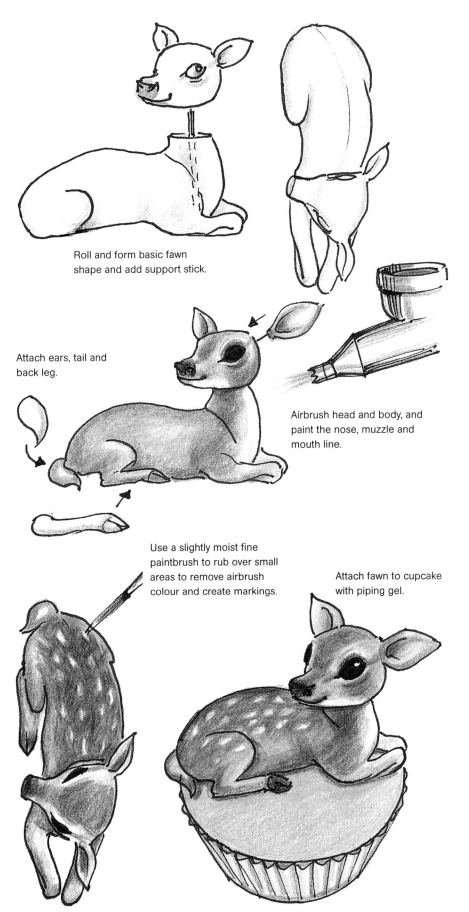

Roll and form basic fawn shape and add support stick.

Attach ears, tail and back leg.

Airbrush head and body, and paint the nose, muzzle and mouth line.

Use a slightly moist fine paintbrush to rub over small areas to remove airbrush colour and create markings.

Attach fawn to cupcake with piping gel.

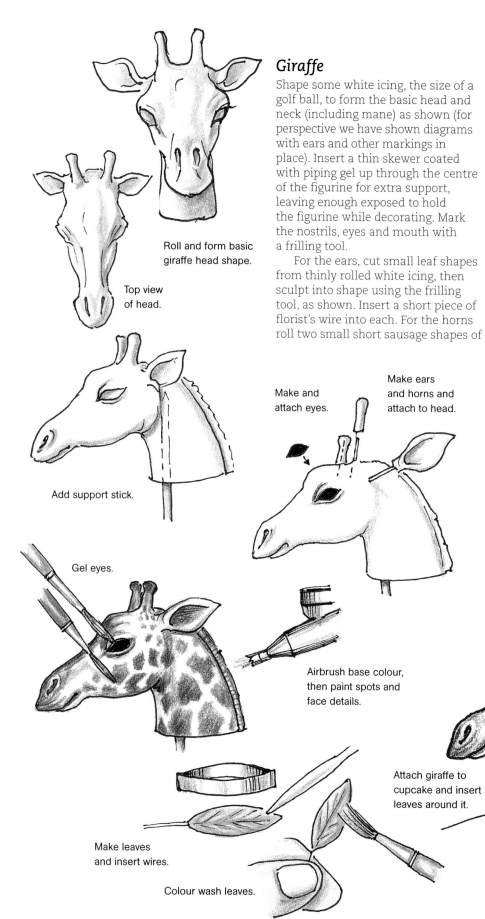

Giraffe

Shape some white icing, the size of a golf ball, to form the basic head and neck (including mane) as shown (for perspective we have shown diagrams with ears and other markings in place). Insert a thin skewer coated with piping gel up through the centre of the figurine for extra support, leaving enough exposed to hold the figurine while decorating. Mark the nostrils, eyes and mouth with a frilling tool.

For the ears, cut small leaf shapes from thinly rolled white icing, then sculpt into shape using the frilling tool, as shown. Insert a short piece of florist's wire into each. For the horns roll two small short sausage shapes of white icing. For the eyes roll two small balls of black icing. Attach the ears, horns and eyes with a dab of water or piping gel.

Airbrush the giraffe's face and neck with brown colour using the photograph (see page 179) as a guide. Paint the giraffe's spots, nose, muzzle, mouth line, horn tips and ear shadow with brown and black colour pastes mixed with alcohol as shown.

For the leaves, use a cutter to cut about 12 leaf shapes from thinly rolled pale olive icing. Mark the veins using a frilling tool. Insert florist's wire into the end of each. Colour wash the leaf veins with dark green colour paste mixed with alcohol. Dry the figurine and leaves overnight.

Cover a cupcake with green icing, then lightly airbrush the edge with brown colour, if desired. Attach the figurine to the cupcake with piping gel. Gel giraffe's eyes and paint white-white colour paste highlights. Insert leaves into cupcake as shown.

Roll and form basic giraffe head shape.

Top view of head.

Add support stick.

Make and attach eyes.

Make ears and horns and attach to head.

Gel eyes.

Airbrush base colour, then paint spots and face details.

Paint eye highlights.

Make leaves and insert wires.

Colour wash leaves.

Attach giraffe to cupcake and insert leaves around it.

Llama

Shape some white icing, the size of a golf ball, to form the basic neck and head as shown (for perspective our diagrams have ears and other markings in place). Insert a thin skewer coated with piping gel through the centre of the figurine for extra support, leaving enough exposed to hold the figurine while decorating. Use a frilling tool to mark nostrils, eyes, mouth and hair.

Shape two small pieces of white icing into long ovals, then sculpt into the ear shape as shown, using frilling tool and your fingers. Insert a short piece of florist's wire into each. Attach to the head with a small dab of water or piping gel. Shape two small balls of black icing for the eyes and attach.

Airbrush the llama's face and neck with ivory colour using the photograph (see page 179) as a guide. Paint the llama's nose, muzzle, mouth line and ear shadow with brown and black colour pastes mixed with alcohol. Dry figurine overnight.

Cover a cupcake with pale brown icing and lightly airbrush the edge with brown colour. Attach the figurine to the cupcake with piping gel. Gel the eyes and paint white-white colour paste highlights. For the scarf, cut three longer strips and one short strip of thinly rolled hot-pink icing. Shred one end of two longer strips with a sharp knife to make tassels. Wrap the remaining longer strip around the llama's neck, trimming if necessary to meet at the side. Attach strips with tassels at the join, shaping as desired. Cover join with the short strip of icing to form a knot. Paint bright stripes using colours of your choice mixed with white-white colour paste.

Roll and form basic llama shape and add support stick.

Top view of head.

Make and attach ears.

Make and attach eyes.

Airbrush face and neck with ivory colour.

Make and attach scarf and paint bright stripes.

Attach llama to cupcake with gel. Then gel eyes and add highlights.

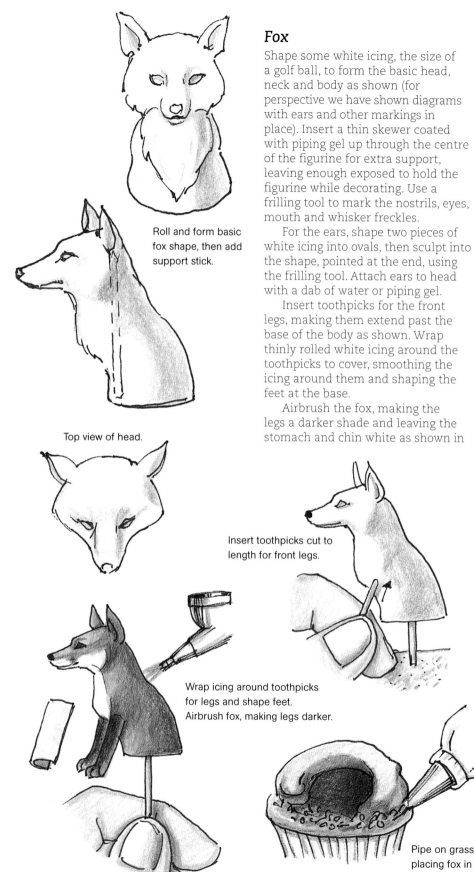

Fox

Shape some white icing, the size of a golf ball, to form the basic head, neck and body as shown (for perspective we have shown diagrams with ears and other markings in place). Insert a thin skewer coated with piping gel up through the centre of the figurine for extra support, leaving enough exposed to hold the figurine while decorating. Use a frilling tool to mark the nostrils, eyes, mouth and whisker freckles.

For the ears, shape two pieces of white icing into ovals, then sculpt into the shape, pointed at the end, using the frilling tool. Attach ears to head with a dab of water or piping gel.

Insert toothpicks for the front legs, making them extend past the base of the body as shown. Wrap thinly rolled white icing around the toothpicks to cover, smoothing the icing around them and shaping the feet at the base.

Airbrush the fox, making the legs a darker shade and leaving the stomach and chin white as shown in photograph (see page 179). Paint the fox's nose, muzzle, mouth line and ear shadow with brown and black colour pastes mixed with alcohol. For the eyes, shape two small balls of orange/brown icing. Attach the eyes with a dab of water or piping gel and paint the centre with black colour paste mixed with alcohol as shown. Dry the figurine overnight.

To make the fox's den, shape a small plum-sized piece of light brown icing making sure the fox's legs will touch the cupcake when sitting in his den. Cover a cupcake with olive green icing. Attach the den to the cupcake with piping gel. Lightly airbrush the edge of the cupcake and den with brown and green colours, making the inside of the den darker as shown. Using a No. 2 plain piping tip and dark green royal icing pipe the grassy foliage around the den. Brush base of the fox with piping gel and place him into the den, inserting the exposed skewer to secure. Gel the eyes and nose. Paint the eye highlights.

Roll and form basic fox shape, then add support stick.

Top view of head.

Insert toothpicks cut to length for front legs.

Attach eyes and paint them.

Wrap icing around toothpicks for legs and shape feet. Airbrush fox, making legs darker.

Pipe on grassy foliage before placing fox in his den.

Tiger

Divide some white icing, about the size of a golf ball, in half. Shape one portion to form the basic head as shown (for perspective we have shown diagrams with ears and other markings in place). Mark nostrils, eyes, mouth and whisker freckles with a frilling tool. Shape the remaining portion into the neck and shoulders. Brush a little water or piping gel over the base of the head and top of the neck, then insert a toothpick coated with piping gel up through centre of neck and base of head to secure.

For the ears, roll two small balls of white icing and use the frilling tool to make an indent in the middle of each. Attach to the head with a dab of water or piping gel. Airbrush the tiger with orange, yellow and brown colours, shading using the photograph (see page 179) as a guide, focusing mainly on the T-zone.

Paint the tiger's nose with pink colour paste mixed with alcohol. Paint the stripes and facial features with black colour paste mixed with alcohol. For the eyes, roll two small balls of green icing. Attach with a dab of water or piping gel. Paint pupils with black colour paste mixed with alcohol.

For the leaves, use a cutter to cut about 16 leaf shapes from thinly rolled pale green icing. Mark the veins using a frilling tool. Insert curved florist's wire into each (this will help shape the leaves). Use a dark green colour paste mixed with alcohol to colour wash the leaf veins. Dry the figurine and leaves overnight.

Cover a cupcake with bright green icing and attach the figurine with piping gel. Insert leaves into cupcake around tiger. Gel the eyes and paint white-white colour paste highlights.

Roll and form basic tiger head and body shapes. Add support stick and attach head to body.

Top view of head.

Airbrush tiger with orange, yellow and brown.

Paint on pinkish nose.

Make leaves, mark veins with a frilling tool and insert curved wire.

Colour wash the leaf veins.

Attach tiger with piping gel and insert leaves around it.

Make green icing irises and attach. Paint pupils, then gel and add highlights.

Roll and form basic panda shape and add support stick.

Make and attach eyes.

Make ears, insert wire supports and attach to head.

Top view of head.

Make arms and attach, wrapping around the chest.

Panda

Shape some white icing, about the size of a golf ball, to form the basic body, neck, head and legs as shown (for perspective we have shown diagrams with ears and other markings in place). Insert a toothpick coated with piping gel up through the centre of the figurine for extra support. Make indents for the eyes, mouth and whisker freckles, if desired, with a frilling tool. For the ears, roll two small pieces of white icing into balls. Make an indent in the middle of each ear with a frilling tool, insert wire supports and attach ears to head. For the eyes, roll two small black balls of icing. Attach eyes to the head with a dab of water or piping gel.

Shape two balls of white icing into arms. Attach the arms, wrapping them around the chest and leaving a very small gap to insert the bamboo. Mark the paws with the frilling tool.

Paint the nose, eyes, ears and body markings with black colour paste mixed with alcohol. Dry the figurine overnight.

Cover a cupcake with white icing and airbrush the edge lightly with blue colour. Attach the figurine to the cupcake with piping gel. Gel the eyes and paint white-white colour paste highlights. Place bought ornamental bamboo leaves in the panda's arms.

Gel eyes and paint highlights.

Paint nose, eyes, ears and body markings.

Attach panda to cupcake, and place ornamental bamboo in arms.

Koala

Shape some white icing, about the size of a golf ball, to form the basic body, neck, head and legs as shown (for perspective we have shown diagrams with ears and other markings in place). Shape the feet by using a small pair of scissors to separate the claws, then smooth with your fingers. Insert a toothpick coated with piping gel up through the centre of the figurine for extra support. Make indents for the eyes, nose, mouth and chest hair with a frilling tool.

For the ears, roll two small pieces of white icing into balls. Make an indent in the middle of each ear, then shape the edges to resemble fur. For the eyes, roll two small brown balls of icing. Attach the ears and eyes to the head with a dab of piping gel or water. Shape two small balls of white icing into arms as shown, shaping the hands and claws with a frilling tool and scissors. Attach the arms, wrapping them around the chest, resting them on the legs and joining the hands so they can hold a flower.

Paint the eye pupil and nose with black colour paste mixed with alcohol. Paint the chin and inside of the nose with pink colour paste mixed with alcohol. Paint around the eyes and inside the ears with light brown colour paste mixed with alcohol. Paint the head and body with grey colour paste mixed with alcohol using the photograph (see page 178) as a guide, leaving the chin, chest and outer part of ear white. Dry figurine overnight.

Cover a cupcake with pale olive green icing and airbrush the edge lightly with brown colour. Attach the figurine to the cupcake with piping gel. Gel the eyes and paint white-white colour paste highlights. Place the small sugar flower into the koala's hands.

Roll and form basic koala shape and add support stick.

Top view of head.

Attach eyes and paint pupils.

Shape and attach arms.

Attach koala to cupcake and place flower in hands.

Paint head and body, leaving some areas white.

Paint chin and inside nose pink.

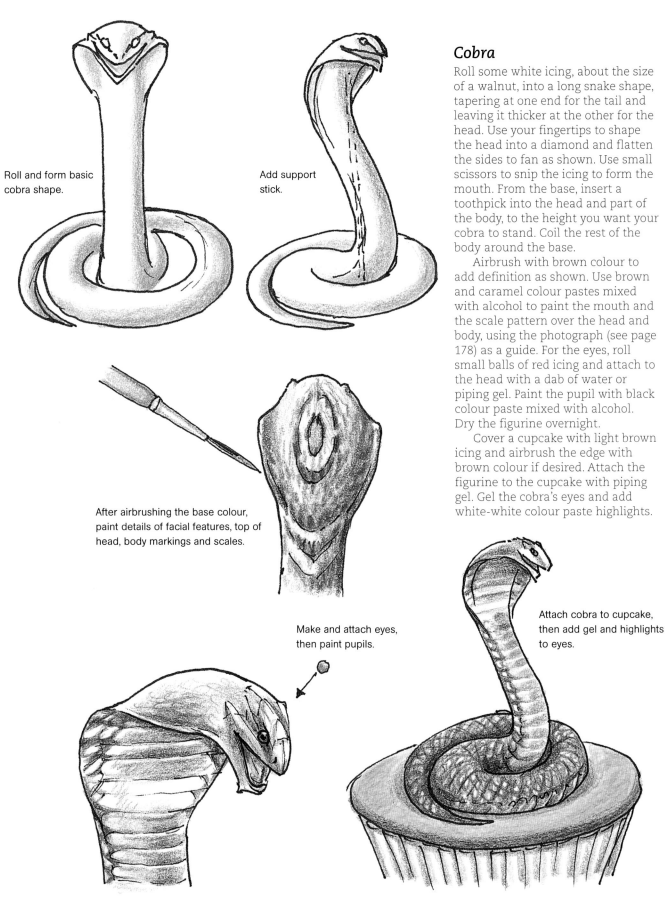

Roll and form basic cobra shape.

Add support stick.

After airbrushing the base colour, paint details of facial features, top of head, body markings and scales.

Make and attach eyes, then paint pupils.

Attach cobra to cupcake, then add gel and highlights to eyes.

Cobra

Roll some white icing, about the size of a walnut, into a long snake shape, tapering at one end for the tail and leaving it thicker at the other for the head. Use your fingertips to shape the head into a diamond and flatten the sides to fan as shown. Use small scissors to snip the icing to form the mouth. From the base, insert a toothpick into the head and part of the body, to the height you want your cobra to stand. Coil the rest of the body around the base.

Airbrush with brown colour to add definition as shown. Use brown and caramel colour pastes mixed with alcohol to paint the mouth and the scale pattern over the head and body, using the photograph (see page 178) as a guide. For the eyes, roll small balls of red icing and attach to the head with a dab of water or piping gel. Paint the pupil with black colour paste mixed with alcohol. Dry the figurine overnight.

Cover a cupcake with light brown icing and airbrush the edge with brown colour if desired. Attach the figurine to the cupcake with piping gel. Gel the cobra's eyes and add white-white colour paste highlights.

Penguin

Shape some white icing, about the size of a walnut, to form the basic body, neck and head as shown (for perspective we have shown diagrams with flippers in place). To form the beak, pull a little of the icing into a point, cut with a small pair of scissors to open it, then use your fingers to shape. Insert a toothpick coated with piping gel up through the centre of the figurine for extra support. Make indents for the eyes with a frilling tool.

Use white icing to shape the flippers and feet. Insert florist's wire into the base of both flippers. Mark the feet with a frilling tool. Attach the flippers and feet to the body with a dab of water or piping gel.

Paint inside the mouth with pink colour paste mixed with alcohol. Paint the head and body with black colour paste mixed with alcohol as shown. Paint the feet with grey colour paste mixed with alcohol.

For the eyes, roll two small balls of white icing and attach to the head with piping gel or a dab of water. Paint the pupil black.

Using white icing, shape a small fish and insert a small length of florist's wire. Make an indent for the eyes with the frilling tool and cut the mouth open with a small knife. Shape teeth from white icing using fingertips and a small knife and attach with piping gel. Paint the fish with colours of your choice. For the eyes, roll tiny balls of white icing and attach with a dab of water or piping gel. Gel the eyes, then paint white-white colour paste highlights. Dry the figurine and fish overnight.

Cover a cupcake with white icing and airbrush the edge lightly with blue colour, if desired. Use a small sharp knife to cut a small hole in the icing, slightly larger than the base of the fish. Use a No. 3 piping tip to pipe blue-coloured piping gel into the hole. Attach the penguin and fish to the cupcake with a little piping gel, and add gel highlights.

Roll and form basic penguin shape and add support stick.

Top view of head.

Paint inside of mouth pink.

Attach eyes and paint pupils.

Paint head and body black, leaving belly and underside of flippers white.

Make and attach flippers and feet.

Paint fish with gel.

Indent eyes with frilling tool.

Attach eyes and teeth.

Paint fish, and gel and highlight eyes.

Cut small hole in icing and pipe in blue gel, then insert fish.

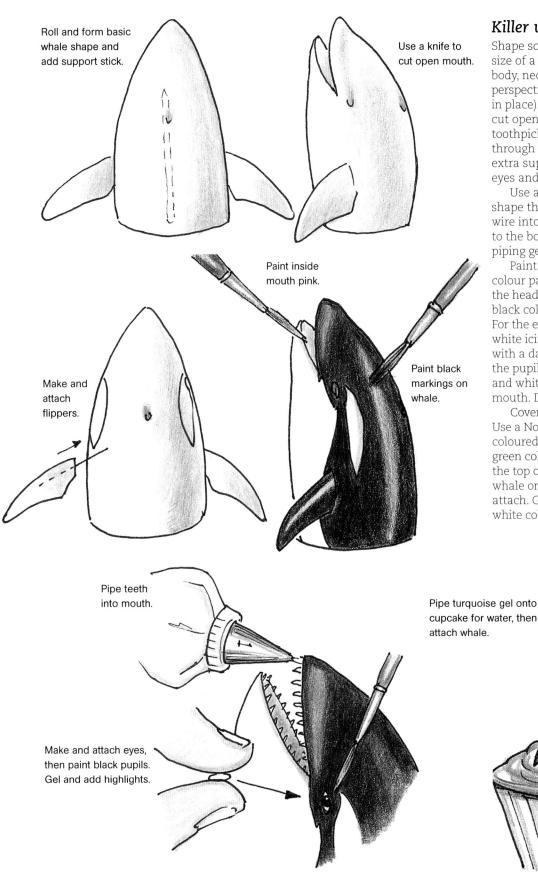

Roll and form basic whale shape and add support stick.

Use a knife to cut open mouth.

Paint inside mouth pink.

Make and attach flippers.

Paint black markings on whale.

Pipe teeth into mouth.

Pipe turquoise gel onto cupcake for water, then attach whale.

Make and attach eyes, then paint black pupils. Gel and add highlights.

Killer whale

Shape some white icing, about the size of a golf ball, to form the basic body, neck and head as shown (for perspective our diagrams have flippers in place). Use a small sharp knife to cut open the mouth. Insert a toothpick coated with piping gel up through the centre of the figurine for extra support. Make indents for the eyes and blowhole with a frilling tool.

Use a little more white icing to shape the flippers and insert florist's wire into the base of each. Attach to the body with a dab of water or piping gel, using the wire to secure.

Paint inside the mouth with pink colour paste mixed with alcohol. Paint the head and body markings with black colour paste mixed with alcohol. For the eyes, roll two small balls of white icing and attach to the head with a dab of water or piping gel. Paint the pupil black. Use a No. 1 piping tip and white royal icing to pipe teeth in mouth. Dry the figurine overnight.

Cover a cupcake with white icing. Use a No. 3 piping tip to pipe turquoise-coloured piping gel (using blue and green colour paste) in circles to cover the top of the cupcake. Place the whale on the cupcake in the 'water' to attach. Gel the eyes and paint white-white colour paste highlights.

Dolphin

Shape white icing, about the size of a golf ball, to form the basic body, neck, head and nose as shown (for perspective we have shown diagrams with flippers in place). Insert a toothpick coated with piping gel up through the centre of the figurine for extra support. Make indents for the eyes, blowhole, ears and mouth with a frilling tool.

Use a little white icing to shape the flippers and insert florist's wire into the base of each. Attach flippers to body with a dab of water or piping gel.

Airbrush the head and body with grey colour as shown. Paint mouth with black colour paste mixed with alcohol. For the eyes, roll two small balls of black icing and attach to the head with a dab of water or piping gel. Dry figurine overnight. Cover a cupcake with white icing. Use a No. 3 piping tip to pipe blue-coloured piping gel in circles to cover the top of the cupcake. Place the dolphin on the cupcake in the 'water' to attach. Gel the eyes and paint white-white colour paste highlights.

Roll and form basic dolphin shape and add support stick.

Shape and attach flippers to body.

Pipe blue gel onto cupcake for water, then attach dolphin.

Airbrush head and body grey, leaving belly and underside of flippers white.

Make and attach eyes, then gel and add highlights.

Paint mouth.

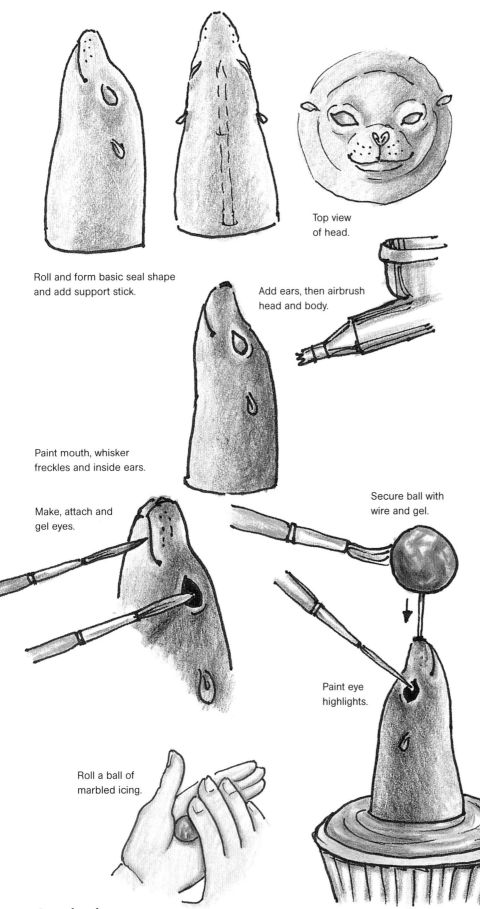

Seal

Shape light brown icing, about the size of a golf ball, to form the basic body, neck, head and nose as shown (for perspective we have shown diagrams with ears and other markings in place). Insert a toothpick coated with piping gel up through the centre of the figurine for extra support. Make indents for the eyes and mouth with a frilling tool.

Shape two small balls of brown icing into ears. Attach to the head with a dab of water or piping gel. Airbrush the head and body with brown colour using, the photograph (see page 179) as a guide. Paint the mouth, whisker freckles and inside the ears with dark brown colour paste mixed with alcohol. For the eyes, roll two small balls of black icing and attach to the head with a dab of water or piping gel.

Roll a small piece of marbled icing, in colours of your choice, into a ball. Insert a piece of florist's wire and attach to the seal's nose. Dry the figurine overnight.

Cover a cupcake with white icing. Use a No. 3 piping tip to pipe blue-coloured piping gel in circles to cover the top of the cupcake. Place the seal on the cupcake in the 'water' to attach. Gel the eyes and paint white-white colour paste highlights. Paint the ball with piping gel.

Roll and form basic seal shape and add support stick.

Top view of head.

Add ears, then airbrush head and body.

Paint mouth, whisker freckles and inside ears.

Make, attach and gel eyes.

Secure ball with wire and gel.

Paint eye highlights.

Roll a ball of marbled icing.

Mix blue gel for water.

Pipe blue gel onto cupcake for water, then attach seal.

Hippopotamus

Shape skin-coloured icing, about the size of a golf ball, to form the basic body, neck, head and snout as shown (for perspective we have shown diagrams with ears and other markings in place). Insert a toothpick coated with piping gel up through the centre of the figurine for extra support. Make indents for the eyes, nostrils, mouth and whisker freckles with a frilling tool.

Shape two very small balls of skin-coloured icing into ears. Attach to the head with a dab of water or piping gel. Airbrush the head and body with brown colour, using the photograph (see page 179) as a guide. Paint the mouth, whisker freckles and inside the ears with dark brown colour paste mixed with alcohol. For the eyes, roll two small balls of black icing and attach to the head with a dab of water or piping gel. Dry the figurine overnight.

Cover a cupcake with light brown icing. Colour a little piping gel with brown and a little white-white colour pastes to create a 'muddy' water colour. Use a No. 3 piping tip to pipe the piping gel in circles to cover the centre of the cupcake. Smooth with a palette knife, if desired. Place the hippo on the cupcake in the 'water' to attach. Gel the eyes and paint white-white colour paste highlights.

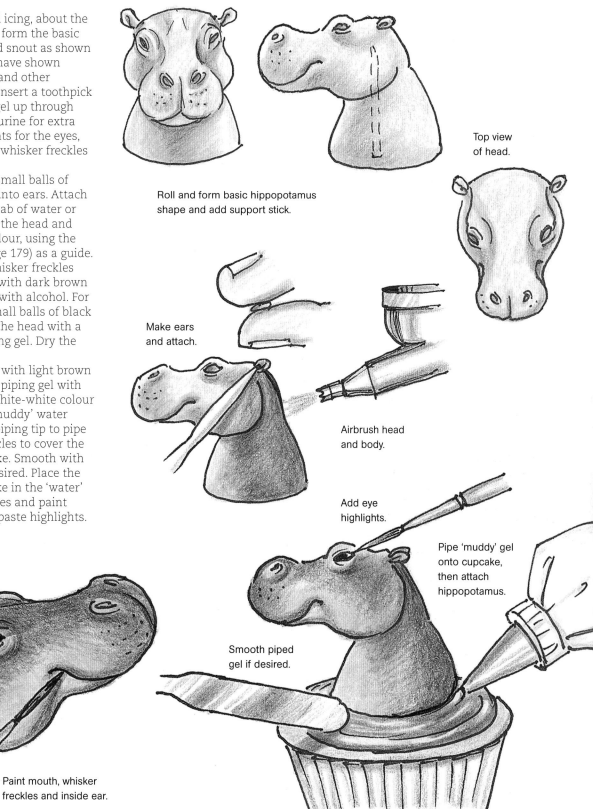

Top view of head.

Roll and form basic hippopotamus shape and add support stick.

Make ears and attach.

Airbrush head and body.

Add eye highlights.

Pipe 'muddy' gel onto cupcake, then attach hippopotamus.

Smooth piped gel if desired.

Paint mouth, whisker freckles and inside ear.

Cupcake how-to

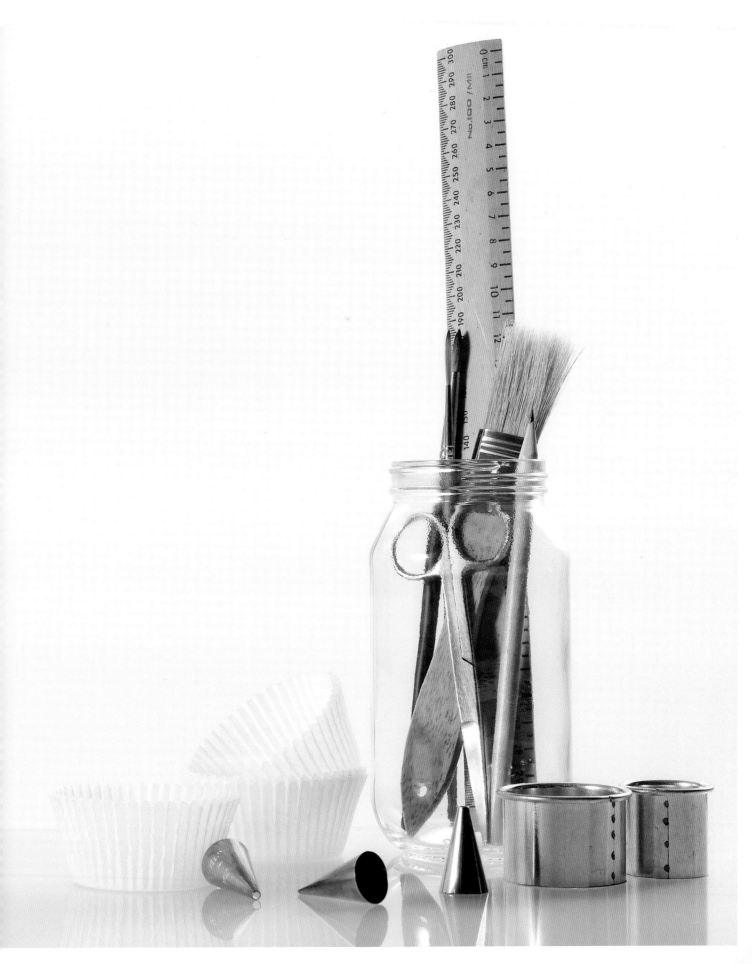

1

3   4   5   6

2

9

11

8

10

7

23

22

24

25

28

32

27

26

31   30   29

Equipment

The best thing about making cupcakes is that the list of equipment and materials required is fairly basic. Most of it can be found either at online cake-decorating specialists or at your local cake-decorating store and much of it may already be in your kitchen or art box. Before you begin, take the time to look at the following lists of equipment and materials that you'll need to start making the cupcakes in this book.

1 Large rolling pin, to roll icing
2 Small rolling pin (or a small piece of dowel), to roll out small pieces of fondant for decorations
3 Cranked palette knife, to spread ganache and to add colour to fondant and royal icing
4 Spatula, to stir ganache and royal icing
5 Pastry brush, to brush cakes with syrup
6 Small sharp knife, to cut out decorations
7 Scissors, to snip fondant for decorations
8 Ruler, to measure cutters, decorations and elements of figurines
9 Flour shaker, for cornflour
10 Circle cutters, to cut cupcake covers and create decorations
11 Shaped cutters, such as flowers (various sizes), small leaf and heart (6 cm/2½ in), to cut out decorations
12 Plastic paint palette
13 Paper butterflies, sugar flowers and silk leaves
14 22-gauge florist's wire
15 Ziplock bags, to store icing
16 Brown florist's tape

17 Synthetic scourer, to mark decorations
18 Leaf mould (optional), for marking veins on leaf decorations
19 A3 paper and tracing paper, to make templates
20 Airbrush machine
21 Glue gun
22 Piping bag
23 No. 1, 2, 3 and 4 piping tips
24 Coupler to attach tips to piping bag (if using material bag)
25 Small star and small leaf (optional) piping tips
26 Small and medium balling tools, to model
27 Frilling tool, to create decorations
28 2B pencil and fine-tip pen, to trace and make templates
29 Fine paintbrush, to paint
30 2 medium paintbrushes, to apply petal dust and to gel and glue decorations
31 Toothpicks, thin wooden skewers, dried spaghetti, and styrofoam balls, to support and mould decorations and figurine parts
32 Flexi-smoother (round-cornered piece of acetate), to smooth icing

1

2

3

8

7

4

5

6

Materials

1 Cupcakes (see recipes, page 204)
2 Syrup, to keep cupcakes moist (see recipe, page 207)
3 White or dark ganache (see recipes, page 206)
4 Royal icing (made from purchased instant powder, or see recipe, page 207)
5 Red and black purchased fondant icing
6 Rolled fondant icing (purchased, or see recipe, page 206)
7 Cornflour, to prevent icing from sticking to bench
8 Tylose powder (hardening agent), to add to fondant when making figurines

9 Red and pink petal dust, for cheek blush
10 Edible silver and gold lustre dust, to add metallic lustre
11 White lustre dust
12 Edible glitter
13 White-white colour paste, for eye highlights and for mixing with other colour pastes
14 Piping gel (also called piping jelly), to add shine to decorations
15 Cake-decorating alcohol, to thin colour paste to paint and to remove stains
16 Airbrush colours
17 Colour paste or liquid, to colour icing and to paint

Recipes

Vanilla cupcakes

Makes 12
Preparation time: 15 minutes
(+ cooling)
Cooking time: 25–30 minutes

175 g (6 oz) butter, at room temperature
165 g (5 ¾ oz/¾ cup) caster
    (superfine) sugar
½ teaspoon natural vanilla extract
2 eggs, at room temperature
110 g (3¾ oz/¾ cup) self-raising flour
150 g (5½ oz/1 cup) plain
    (all-purpose) flour
160 ml (5½ fl oz/⅔ cup) buttermilk

1 Preheat the oven to 180°C (350°F/
   Gas 4). Line the holes of a 12-hole
   80 ml (2½ fl oz/⅓ cup) muffin tin
   with paper cases.

2 Beat the butter, sugar and vanilla
   in a medium bowl using an electric
   mixer until light and fluffy.

3 Beat the eggs into the butter
   mixture one at a time. Add half
   the sifted flours and half the
   buttermilk, and mix on low speed
   until just combined. Mix in the
   remaining flours and buttermilk.

4 Divide the mixture evenly among
   the paper cases. Gently smooth the
   tops (this will help the cupcakes
   rise evenly).

5 Bake for 25–30 minutes or until
   lightly golden and cooked when
   tested with a skewer. Allow cupcakes
   to stand for 5 minutes in tin before
   transferring to a wire rack to cool.

Chocolate cupcakes
Reduce the plain flour to 110 g
(3¾ oz/¾ cup). Sift 30 g (1 oz/¼ cup)
sifted unsweetened cocoa powder
and ¼ teaspoon bicarbonate of soda
(baking soda) with the flours.

Orange poppy seed cupcakes
Replace the vanilla extract with
1 tablespoon finely grated orange
zest. Add 1½ tablespoons poppy
seeds with the sifted flours.

Gluten-free cupcakes

Makes 12
Preparation time: 15 minutes
(+ cooling)
Cooking time: 25–30 minutes

175 g (6 oz) butter, at room temperature
165 g (5 3/4 oz/ 3/4 cup) caster
    (superfine) sugar
1/2 teaspoon natural vanilla extract
2 eggs, at room temperature
140 g (5 oz/1 cup) gluten-free
    self-raising flour
140 g (5 oz/1 cup) gluten-free
    plain (all-purpose) flour
160 ml (5 1/2 fl oz/ 2/3 cup) buttermilk

1 Preheat the oven to 180°C (350°F/
Gas 4). Line the holes of a 12-hole
80 ml (2 1/2 fl oz/ 1/3 cup) muffin tin
with paper cases.

2 Beat the butter, sugar and vanilla
in a medium bowl using an electric
mixer until light and fluffy.

3 Beat the eggs into the butter
mixture one at a time. Add half
the sifted flours and half the
buttermilk, and mix on low speed
until just combined. Mix in the
remaining flours and buttermilk.

4 Divide the mixture evenly among
the paper cases. Gently smooth the
tops (this will help the cupcakes
rise evenly).

5 Bake for 25–30 minutes or until
lightly golden and cooked when
tested with a skewer. Allow cupcakes
to stand for 5 minutes in tin before
transferring to a wire rack to cool.

Cupcake tips

- Start testing the cupcakes 2 minutes before the end of baking time.
  Once they give a light resistance to touch, you can start testing
  them with a toothpick or skewer. The tester must come out clean,
  with absolutely no wet mixture and no crumbs clinging to it.

- Store the vanilla, chocolate and orange poppy seed cupcakes in
  a sealed airtight container in the fridge for up to 3 days, and the
  gluten-free cakes for up to 1 day. All cupcakes can also be frozen for
  up to 3 months. Bring to room temperature before decorating.

Ganache

Makes about 480 g (1 lb 1 oz/ 1¼ cups), enough for 24 cupcakes
Preparation time: 10 minutes
Cooking time: 5 minutes
(+ overnight standing)

The ideal chocolate for making ganache is a couverture variety with a cocoa content of 53–63 per cent. In cold weather, you might have to add a touch more cream so that the ganache doesn't set too hard.

White ganache

325 g (11½ oz) white chocolate, finely chopped
150 ml (5 fl oz) pure cream

Dark ganache

300 g (10½ oz) dark chocolate, finely chopped
150 ml (5 fl oz) pure cream

1 To make either the white or dark ganache, put the chocolate in a medium heat-proof bowl.

2 Put the cream in a saucepan and bring just to a simmer. Pour the cream over the chocolate and stir with a balloon whisk until the ganache is smooth.

3 Cool completely. Cover and leave to firm overnight at room temperature.

Microwave method

1 Put the chocolate and cream in a microwave-safe bowl and heat for 1 minute on HIGH power. Remove from microwave and stir with a balloon whisk. Repeat, heating in 10–20 second bursts, stirring between each, until the ganache is smooth.

2 Cool completely. Cover and leave to firm overnight at room temperature.

Ganache tips

- At Planet Cake, we use either white or dark chocolate ganache under the fondant icing on all our cupcakes. We use white ganache with vanilla and citrus-flavoured cupcakes, and when covering cupcakes with pale-coloured fondant icing; dark ganache on chocolate and nut-based cupcakes. Note that the white is less stable than the dark in hot weather and won't set as firmly.

- Avoid using dark chocolate with a cocoa content of more than 63 per cent to make dark ganache. It is more likely to burn when heated, and separates easily. It may also be too bitter in contrast to the sweet fondant icing, and will set very hard, as it contains very little cocoa butter.

- We use pure cream (single cream), not thickened or thick (double) cream, when making ganache. A cream with a lower fat content (but not low-fat) is best as it won't thicken when mixed.

- Ganache will keep for about 1 week in an airtight container in the fridge, so check the use-by date of the cream you are using.

- Ganache also freezes well if you want to make a large batch of it. Freeze it in small containers so you can thaw just the quantity needed.

- Always bring ganache to room temperature before using.

- If your ganache needs reheating to soften it slightly, place the amount you need in a microwave-safe dish and heat in 5-second bursts on MEDIUM power, stirring between each burst, until it reaches the desired consistency.

- Allow about 20 g (¾ oz) ganache per cupcake.

Fondant icing

Makes about 1.25 kg (2 lb 12 oz)
Preparation time: 15 minutes
Cooking time: 5 minutes

At Planet Cake, we don't make our own fondant icing, as we find the commercial varieties convenient and often more reliable to use. But if you do need a recipe, this one is courtesy of our friend Greg Cleary — a great cake decorator.

15 g (½ oz) powdered gelatine
125 ml (4 fl oz/½ cup) liquid glucose
25 ml (5 teaspoons) glycerine
1 kg (2 lb 4 oz) pure icing sugar
2 drops flavour extract (optional)

1 Sprinkle the gelatine over 60ml (2 fl oz/¼ cup) water in a small heat-proof bowl. Leave to stand for 3 minutes or until the gelatine is spongy.

2 Place the bowl over a saucepan of simmering water and stir until the gelatine dissolves. Add the glucose and glycerine and stir until melted. Strain through a fine sieve if the mixture is lumpy.

3 Sift the icing sugar into a large bowl, make a well in the centre and pour in the warm gelatine mixture. Use a wooden spoon until it becomes too difficult to stir. Tip the mixture out onto a bench, add the flavouring extract, if using, and knead with dry hands for 3–5 minutes or until a smooth, pliable dough forms.

4 Wrap the fondant well in plastic wrap or in a ziplock bag and store in an airtight container in a cool place (but do not refrigerate).

5 Knead again before using, adding a little more sifted pure icing sugar if necessary.

Fondant tips

- Fondant icing can dry out very quickly, so it is important to work quickly to avoid your icing becoming cracked and difficult to use.

- Never use icing that is too dry or over-kneaded; this will make the icing on the cakes crack very easily.

- NEVER EVER refrigerate icing when it is on a cake. Fondant will sweat in the fridge. Once the cupcakes are covered, they should be stored in a cool place (about 20°C/68°F).

- Never ice cupcakes straight from the fridge. For a professional finish, always bring chilled cakes to room temperature before covering.

- When you are not using your icing (even for a minute), put it in a good-quality sealed plastic bag to avoid it drying out. Any excess or leftover icing is best stored the same way or wrapped in plastic wrap and then in a sealed airtight container. Follow the manufacturer's instructions on how to store your particular brand of purchased icing. We store ours at room temperature.

- Hot hands may make your icing sticky. Don't be tempted to over-use cornflour, which will dry the icing. Cool your hands under cold water and keep cornflour to a light sprinkle.

- Weather will also affect fondant icing. Humidity will make the icing sticky and very cold weather will make it as hard as rock.

- Always work the icing in small amounts and try to get above the icing when you knead it on the bench. If you are short, stand on a step stool so you can use your body-weight to help you knead. If you try to knead large amounts of icing, you will put undue pressure on your wrists and make the job very difficult.

- Kneading icing is not like kneading dough: if you keep pummelling it, it will stick to the board and become unmanageable. Treat icing a bit like playdough and keep folding it in until it is smooth and warm to use, but not sticking to the bench.

- To use fondant icing for modelling, knead 1 teaspoon Tylose powder into 500 g (1 lb 2 oz) fondant until thoroughly combined.

Royal icing

Makes about 270 g (9$\frac{1}{2}$ oz/1 cup)
Preparation time: 10 minutes

Achieving the right consistency for royal icing can be difficult. For piping with tubes, you will need 'soft peak' royal icing — when lifted from the bowl with a spatula, the peak will stand up but droop over slightly at the tip, like uncooked meringue.

250–300 g (9–10$\frac{1}{2}$ oz/2–2$\frac{1}{2}$ cups) pure icing sugar, sifted
1 egg white
2–4 drops lemon juice or white vinegar

1 Put 250 g (9 oz/2 cups) icing sugar, egg white and lemon juice or vinegar in a bowl and beat with an electric mixer on medium–high speed for 5 minutes for 'soft peaks' (less if you want it firmer). If too soft, beat in a little more sifted icing sugar.

2 Store in an airtight container in a cool place (but don't refrigerate) for up to 4 days.

Syrup

Makes about 160 ml (5$\frac{1}{4}$ fl oz/$\frac{2}{3}$ cup)
Preparation time: 5 minutes

105 g (3$\frac{3}{4}$ oz/$\frac{1}{3}$ cup) apricot jam
2 teaspoons orange liqueur (optional)

1 Whisk the jam with 100 ml (3$\frac{1}{2}$ fl oz) boiling water until smooth.

2 Strain through a fine sieve to remove any lumps. Stir in the liqueur, if using.

Techniques

Ganaching cupcakes

At Planet Cake, we ganache our cupcakes to help extend their life span and ensure that they are moist and delicious. Ganache also builds up the surface of the cupcakes, so that they are all perfectly uniform in spite of any imperfections that may have happened during the baking process.

1 Make your ganache (page 206) and allow it to stand overnight at room temperature to firm. If the ganache is too hard when you are ready to use it, heat it in short bursts in the microwave until it reaches the consistency of smooth peanut butter. If you don't have a microwave, put the ganache in a saucepan over low heat, stirring constantly and making sure not to heat it too much.

2 Trim the cupcake tops (optional). If your cupcakes have spilled over their paper cases during baking or are uneven, trim the tops with a sharp knife to make sure they all have a similar height and proportion. Keep in mind it is very difficult to ice a high-domed cupcake, so make sure they are not too high. For the mosaic designs (pages 60–93), the cupcakes are best trimmed so that the tops are completely level.

3 Brush the top of the cupcakes liberally with syrup (page 207). This will help to prevent them from drying out (Pic a).

4 Using a palette knife, spread approximately 2 teaspoons of ganache across the top of the cupcake, being careful not to touch the paper case, particularly if you are using dark ganache (Pics b, c).

a

b

c

d

5 Allow the ganache to become firm to the touch before covering with fondant icing (Pic d). If it is a warm day you can place your cakes in the fridge for about 5 minutes.

Tips

- When estimating the total amount of ganache needed for covering your cakes, you should allow about 20 g (¾ oz) ganache per cupcake.
- Before covering the cupcakes with fondant icing, the ganache should feel firm to the touch. If it is a warm day, you can speed up the setting time by placing your cake in the fridge for about 5 minutes.

Timing guideline

At Planet Cake, we follow the following timing guideline when covering our cupcakes:

1 Bake your cupcakes and allow to cool (at least 30 minutes). They can be frozen at this stage.

2 Trim and ganache cupcakes.

3 Set aside for 4 hours or until ganache is firm to the touch.

4 Cover with fondant icing and decorate.

Covering cupcakes

It is very important to learn how to cover cupcakes professionally — practice makes perfect. By the time you have covered a few batches of cupcakes, they will start to look better than most of the cupcakes you can buy commercially. Don't be put off by a bumpy first attempt.

First ganache your cupcakes and check that the ganache is firm before you attempt to cover the cupcakes with rolled fondant. The better the ganache preparation, the better the finished cupcakes will look.

1 Wipe your bench clean and make sure it is dry. Knead the fondant icing to a pliable dough, using just a sprinkle of cornflour if it sticks. Making sure the icing is smooth, roll it into a ball and flatten it with the palm of your hand to about 4 cm (1½ in) thick.

2 Sprinkle some cornflour on your bench and roll out the icing, starting from the centre and rolling a couple of times in one direction. Turn the icing, and repeat the process. If your bench gets sticky, use a bit more cornflour, but never use cornflour on top of the icing. Keep on rolling and turning this way until the icing is about 3 mm (⅛ in) thick.

3 Use a cutter the same size as, or slightly larger than, your cupcakes to cut out the number of discs you need to cover the cakes (Pic a). At Planet Cake, we use a 7 cm (2¾ in) round cutter. Cover the discs with plastic wrap to prevent them from drying out while cutting out the remainder.

4 Working with one cupcake at a time, brush the ganached cake all over with syrup (page 207). This will help the fondant stick (Pic b).

5 Turn one of the icing discs over and use your fingertip to smooth the edge (Pic c).

a

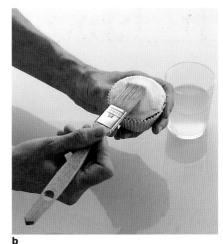

b

c

d

6 Turn the disc the right way up and place on top of the cupcake. Gently manipulate the icing so it sits perfectly on the surface of the cupcake (Pic d).

7 Use a flexi-smoother to smooth the icing disc (Pic e).

Tip

It is possible to decorate some cupcake discs in advance of covering the cake. Follow all of the instructions for covering a cupcake, with the exception of placing the cover on the cake. Decorate the discs separately and place them on the cupcake later if you wish, following the same instructions for placing them. This technique only works if you have flat cupcake tops, such as those for Mosaics; it does not work for domed cupcakes.

e

Colouring fondant icing

The important thing to remember when colouring icing to cover cupcakes is to add just a little of the concentrated icing colour at a time, until you arrive at the exact shade you want. Always make sure you have enough coloured icing for all your cupcakes, as matching the original colour can sometimes be an impossible task!

a

b

1 Begin with a kneadable amount of white fondant icing, the concentrated icing colour and disposable gloves (Pic a). There are many different brands and types of icing colour and it is easy to become confused. We recommend an icing colour paste, rather than liquid, to colour rolled fondant icing. The gloves are optional, but will keep your hands stain-free.

2 Add a dot of colour to the fondant. Using a toothpick or palette knife, add small dots of icing colour at a time. You can make more elaborate colours by mixing different icing colours together (Pic b). We suggest using a colour wheel as a guide.

3 Knead in the colour paste until the colour is evenly blended, adding a little more colour if needed (Pics c, d). The best way to test whether the colour is blended is to cut the icing in half; it should not be a swirl, but rather a solid colour all the way through.

Intense colours

When making deep colours, such as black, brown, red, orange or royal blue, use icing colour pastes or liquids in larger amounts than normal. It is best to make coloured icing the day before it is needed. The icing will be exceptionally soft (due both to the large amount of colour pigment needed and the amount of kneading required to thoroughly blend it in), so standing it overnight will help firm it up, making it easier to work with. (See also Red and black icing, opposite.)

c

d

Fading

After the icing is coloured, you need to protect the colours from fading. Pinks, purples and blues are especially susceptible to fading out, even in a couple of hours. Pink and mauve can be reduced to almost white when exposed to sunlight; purples to blues; blues to grey. Be careful to protect the icing from light, by covering the cakes with a cloth or placing them in a cake box.

a

b

c

Red and black icing

Red- and black-coloured icing can be difficult to make and challenging to work with, because so much colour pigment is required to make an intense colour. In addition, once the icing is coloured successfully, it is very soft and sticky due to the amount of colour required to make it.

To avoid sticky icing, always make red or black icing the day before using it, to allow the colour to be absorbed and the icing to harden. If the icing is still too soft and keeps sticking to the bench, knead in a little sifted icing sugar to dry it out a little.

1 To make the colour, you will need purchased pre-coloured black or red fondant, the same amount of white fondant and possibly some colouring paste. We find the pre-coloured icing unmanageable on its own, as it is too soft and has too much pigment, therefore we dilute it with white fondant.

2 Start by mixing pre-coloured red or black icing and white fondant icing in a 50/50 ratio (Pic a). To get the intense colour you desire, you may also need to add some colour paste (Pic b). Do this after you have mixed the icing and gradually top up the colour until you reach the desired intensity, kneading it in well (Pic c).

Tip

One of our tricks at Planet Cake is to use a pasta machine for rolling out icing. It can be easier than using a traditional rolling pin to get an even thickness. Make sure you knead and roll the icing out first, with a small rolling pin, before feeding it into the pasta machine. And remember to keep the machine clean, especially after using strong colours.

Skin-coloured icing

Make skin-coloured icing by starting with a small ball of white fondant icing and mixing in the appropriate icing colours (see below), drop by drop, until you have the shade you desire (Pics a, b). Remember that you need very little of each colour, so be sparing — you can always add a little more, if needed. If you are making a figurine, you can also add Tylose powder (see Glossary) to the fondant before you start colouring.

PINK SKIN Mix red, yellow and brown in equal amounts into white fondant.

OLIVE SKIN Add more yellow and brown to pink skin.

BROWN SKIN Add more brown to pink skin.

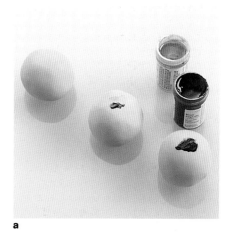

a

b

Marbling

Marbling is a simple technique that creates an effective swirled pattern in the fondant.

1 Start with two small portions of fondant icing in different colours of your choice. Roll each portion of fondant into a rope and then twist them together (Pic a).

2 Roll the twisted rope into a ball in the palm of your hands (Pic b). Take care not to over-knead it or the colours will fuse into a single shade.

3 Flatten the ball slightly. Sprinkle your work surface with a little cornflour and roll out the fondant to the desired thickness (Pic c).

4 Cut out shapes and use as desired (Pic d).

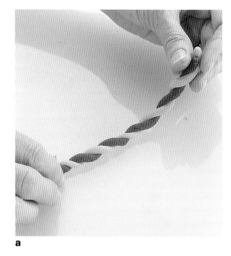

a

b

c

d

Gluing icing

There is nothing fancy about gluing icing together, but it can be confusing. Icing is made of sugar and so will readily 'glue' to itself with water alone. You can also use piping gel (see page 213) instead of water; apply water or gel using a paintbrush when gluing decorations, to be more accurate. You can also use a dab of royal icing, but it should be the same colour as the fondant it is being applied to, and used very sparingly.

1 Make a very light line or dab of water or gel where the icing needs to be glued (Pic a).

2 Hold the icing piece in place for a few minutes to see if it sets. A small sharp utensil to hold and press together is useful for very small pieces/body parts (Pic b).

Always use a dab of water or gel to secure one piece of icing to another, even when you are also using a skewer or wire for support.

If you haven't applied enough water or gel, you can always add a little more, but if you apply too much, you may end up with a sodden mess.

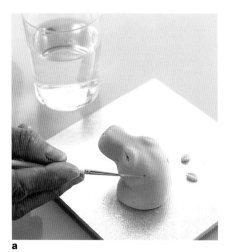

a

b

Edible painting and colour wash

Use colour pastes, cake-decorating alcohol and fine or medium paintbrushes for both painting and colour washing.

For colour washing (Pic a), dilute the colour paste to a thin wash with alcohol using about twice the amount of alcohol that is needed for painting. Work with small quantities and work quickly as the 'wash', being alcohol-based, dries almost instantly.

For painting (Pic b), dilute a small amount of colour paste with alcohol to the desired consistency.

Test the paint or wash on a piece of icing first and keep adding either colour paste or alcohol until you get the intensity of colour you want. We recommend painting on white or light-coloured icing.

a

b

Gelling

Translucent piping gel gives surfaces a shiny appearance. It can be used over coloured fondant, just as it comes, on features such as eyes or noses, to make them look shiny and 'alive', or colouring paste can be added to achieve a depth of colour for liquids, such as tea (Pic a), and for water effects. We usually just brush it on with a pastry brush or paintbrush.

However, if you want a thick, even coating (as for the tea in the cup for the Fairy tea party), then pipe it onto the surface through a small piping nozzle (Pic b) and smooth it with a palette knife (Pic c), if desired.

Piping gel is also sometimes labelled as piping jelly and is available from cake-decorating suppliers.

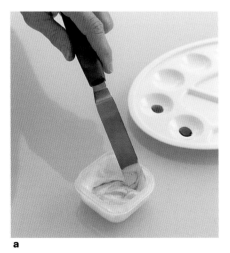

a

b

c

Painting in silver and gold

a

For this technique, you will need edible silver or gold lustre dust, which can be found in nearly all cake-decorating supply stores.

Mix the dust with cake-decorating alcohol and then, using a fine paintbrush, apply it to the icing (Pic a).

As they are very fine, silver and gold dust can spread everywhere and contaminate your cakes and decorations. Be sure to place paper underneath your project when using the dust and, if you are painting directly onto the cake itself, try to cover unpainted areas of the cake with paper before proceeding.

Edible glitter

Non-toxic edible glitter is available from cake-decorating supply stores and is easy to apply.

1 Trace over the area where you wish to apply the glitter with a paintbrush coated with water, piping gel or syrup (see page 207) (Pic b).

2 Dust the wet area with edible glitter and wait until dry (Pic c).

3 Dust away the excess glitter with a perfectly dry, soft brush (Pic d).

c

b

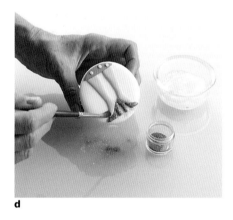

d

Blush

To create rosy cheeks, mix red and pink petal dust to the desired colour in a small container, then use a dry fine paintbrush to rub it in (Pic e). Use this paintbrush only for applying blush, as the rubbing will divide the bristles and the brush will no longer be suitable for fine painting work. Alternatively, you can use a small make-up brush.

e

Eyes

Well-executed eyes can make your cupcakes look professional — as well as adding character to each face. It's not difficult to paint life-like eyes: choose the appropriate technique and follow the simple steps. Piping gel is an important part of each technique; it keeps the eyes bright and shiny.

Eye 1

(MIX-N-MATCH BETTY SUE; PLAYFUL PUPPIES; DINOSAUR EGGS; SOME SAVE THE PLANET ANIMALS) Roll a small ball of black icing and flatten slightly. Paint with piping gel. When dry, add a dot of white-white colour paste for highlight (Pic a).

Eye 2

(SOME BAD-MANNERED MONSTERS; SAVE THE PLANET: TIGER) Roll a small ball of chosen eye colour and flatten slightly. Paint with piping gel. Paint black pupil and apply more gel. Paint white-white highlight dot (Pic b).

Eye 3

(BABIES; SANTA'S CREW: SANTA & ELVES) Roll a small ball of black icing and flatten slightly. Paint with piping gel. Use white-white colour paste to paint two highlight dots, one larger than the other (Pic c).

Eye 4

(BAD-MANNERED MONSTERS: NAUGHTY BOY AND GREEN MONSTER; SOME SAVE THE PLANET ANIMALS) Roll a small ball of white icing and flatten slightly. Paint the iris with your chosen colour. Paint black pupil and outline the iris with black. When dry, paint with piping gel. Paint white-white highlight (Pic d).

Placing human eyes

e

As a rough guide, place the eyes for babies about one-third of the way up their face. As a child grows, the facial features 'move up' the face as teeth develop and the jaw grows to accommodate these. By the time children lose their baby fat in the pre- or early teen years, their eyes will have moved midway up the face (Pic e).

a

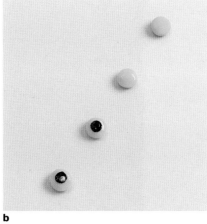

b

c

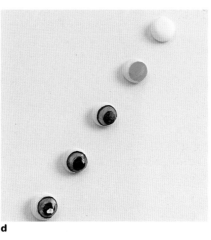

d

Airbrushing

Airbrushing is a technique in which edible liquid paints are sprayed through a needle tip, using compressed air from a machine. It is one of the quickest and easiest ways to add colour to a cake. If you plan on decorating cakes regularly, it's probably worth investing in a good airbrushing system designed for cakes. You will also need to buy specific airbrush colours for the machine as normal icing liquid colours and pastes will ruin it.

If you are using a deep colour, start with a lighter shade of icing as your base colour, then airbrush darker. For example, for shading a hippo, start with a skin-colour base shade, then airbrush brown, leaving skin-coloured areas around the mouth, chin and chest, around the eyes, and in the ears.

1 Fill the airbrush reservoir three-quarters full with the first colour you need (Pic a). You will also need to add cake-decorating alcohol if subtle shading is required.

2 Practise airbrushing on a piece of extra fondant. This allows you to check that the nozzle isn't blocked and that the colour tone is correct. You will also be able to work out how heavily you'll need to airbrush to get the desired effect. Point the airbrush nozzle at the icing surface and gently press the trigger. Keep the nozzle at a 45 degree angle, no more than 20 cm (8 in) from the surface (Pic b). Sweep the machine across the surface while spraying, to make soft swathes of colour.

3 Now airbrush the cupcake or figurine to the desired depth of colour (Pic c).

4 A great effect can be achieved by airbrushing layers of different colours. Apply a light covering of the lightest colour first (Pic d). Now add a second layer with a deeper colour, allowing the lighter colour to show through where desired

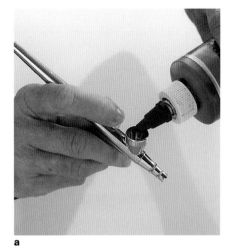

a

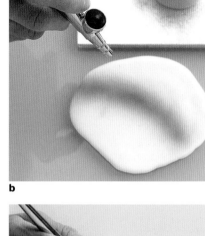

b

c

d

e

f

(Pic e). Then airbrush the darkest colour around the edges. When airbrushing near the paper case, hold a paper mask (page 98) between the cupcake icing and paper case while airbrushing (Pic f).

5 Always clean airbrush equipment (including all piping) with cold water directly after use and between each change of paint colours.

Piping with royal icing

You can make royal icing from scratch (see page 207) or buy instant royal icing, which is a good substitute. To make up the instant icing, simply mix the powder with water, as directed on the packet.

Before piping with royal icing, it is essential to have it at the correct consistency — not too runny and not too thick, as it will keep blocking the piping tip and drive you crazy! An ideal consistency is about the same as uncooked meringue, when it is just holding soft peaks.

1 If you wish to colour your royal icing, add icing colour paste in very small quantities. Mix the royal icing and colour together using a palette knife or spoon (Pic a). You can also use liquid or gel icing colour. Use a toothpick to add colour paste and remember, a little will go a long way.

2 At Planet Cake, we make our piping bags from parchment paper because we pipe all day long. However, disposable plastic and material icing bags are perfect for home decorating. Place the piping tip in the piping bag. Remember that if you have a material bag, you will also need a coupler to attach the piping tip to the bag.

3 Only fill the piping bag one-third full with royal icing (Pic b). If you find it difficult to hold the bag and fill it at the same time, you can steady the bag in a glass while you fill it. Make sure that the icing is pushed down towards the piping end of the bag and give it a few squeezes to get rid of any air pockets. Then twist the end of the bag to seal.

4 If you have never piped anything before, the best way to practise is to pipe some icing lines. Grasp the bag correctly, squeezing with one hand and steadying your arm with the other hand, if necessary. Hold the piping bag at a 45 degree angle

a

b

c

d

just above the work surface and apply pressure to see the icing emerge from the tip. Touch the end of the icing thread to the surface, then pipe along, allowing the thread to fall into place, creating a line. If you move the tip slightly from side to side, you will create a wavy line (Pic c). When you feel confident, use the same technique on the surface of a covered cupcake (Pic d).

Royal icing tips

• A coupler attaches the piping tip to the bag and is needed for material bags.

• The round piping tips used for royal icing come in an assortment of sizes, from No. 00 to No. 12. The numbers correspond with the size of the hole, No. 00 being the smallest. A No. 1 piping tip or smaller can be a little frustrating for beginners, so start with a No. 2 tip or bigger and gradually work your way up to fine piping. If you are only piping in royal icing (as we do) and not using butter cream, you will only need a couple of round piping tips to start. Star- or leaf-shaped tips are optional, although we do occasionally use a star tip.

Figurine modelling

Once you understand the basic principles behind modelling, you should be able to make whatever figurines or animals you wish. Here are the principles we use at Planet Cake.

Timing

It is advisable to make the figurines at least a day before you decorate your cakes, in order to allow drying time. However, figurines can be made weeks in advance, and this is what we would recommend — it is much more enjoyable to make them without the pressure of a deadline.

Hardening

When making figurines, you need to mix Tylose powder into the fondant icing to ensure that it dries very hard. You need to add about 1 teaspoon for every 500 g (1 lb 2 oz oz) of icing. However, if you need a smaller quantity, it doesn't need to be an exact science — you can just lightly roll a golf ball-sized piece of icing in Tylose powder and then mix it in (Pic a). Always remember, you can add more, but you cannot take away.

Modelling theory

The theory behind traditional marzipan modelling is that everything starts from a ball. The same principle applies to figurine modelling with fondant icing: if you start with a ball, you have the best starting position for any shape you need to create. It also ensures that you have kneaded the icing and it is warm and free of cracks. Therefore, we recommend starting from a ball for all your different elements (Pic b).

Support

Use thin bamboo skewers or toothpicks to support heads, limbs and standing figures (Pic c). If the cupcake is intended for a small child, be sure to use dried spaghetti instead of these non-edible items. Leave a short length of the support material extending from the moulded icing, so it can be inserted into the cupcake (Pic d). Use water or piping gel in addition to the supports to stick limbs and heads on. Styrofoam balls are great to use as a base support for round shapes, such as the teapot in the Fairy tea party.

Painting

For painting, use either liquid colour, icing colour paste or, if airbrushing, airbrush colour, diluted with cake-decorating alcohol. When using an airbrush or painting your figurines, always make the figurine in its lightest colour or a contrasting colour that will intensify the final shade. For example, the Tyrannosaurus from the Dinosaur eggs story (page 151) was made with yellow fondant icing and then airbrushed with neon green, and then darker green, to create the desired final colour and effect (Pic e).

a

b

c

d

e

Where to start

HUMAN FIGURINES It is really important to start with the head and then to make the body to suit. The reason for this is that it is very difficult to estimate the proportions of the head in advance, before you have sculpted the facial features.

ANIMAL FIGURINES Some animal bodies and heads can be made in one piece, with arms, paws, flippers and so on (where applicable) to be added later (such as the dinosaurs in Dinosaur eggs). Therefore, you will need to start with the body. However, if the head can be made separately, or if it is very detailed, it is best to make the head and body separately and join them later.

Child/fairy proportions

The body proportions of children are quite different to those of adults. When they are born, babies' heads are extremely large in proportion to the rest of their body. As a child grows, the head becomes smaller in proportion to their body (Pic a).

The head of a very young child makes up about one-quarter of its total height until it is about six or seven, when the head is about one-sixth of the height. A child's head is wider than it is long, so it's rounder than that of an adult. The facial features of a baby take up a very small part of the head, with the eyebrows at about midway between crown and chin. There is almost no chin and the nose is not prominent.

Humans are born with eyeballs at almost adult size, so a baby's eyes appear very large compared to the other features. Very little of the white of the eyes is visible. Paint the faces with colour paste mixed with cake-decorating alcohol, using the finest paintbrush possible. For realistic figurines, such as the fairy (Pic b), outline the lips with dark pink, and then fill in the lip colour. Add a tiny white dot at the same side of the pupil on each eye, to indicate light reflection.

a

b

c

d

Animal elements

When modelling animals and birds, it is always easier to work from a reference: plastic animals, illustrations and photographs are the perfect guide (Pic c).

Break an animal down into elements, beginning with the body. For example, a dog can be broken down easily. Body, pear-shape; Head, triangle with rounded corners; Ears, 2 leaves; Snout, lopsided half-sphere; Legs, stumpy sausages; Tail, small sausage with a tip (Pics d, e).

Tip

Children are most attracted to animals that are animated; for example, a dog playing with a toy, rather than simply sitting.

e

Making simple moulds

Learning how to make moulds is invaluable for any cake decorator. Not only can you save money, but you can also create something unique. This technique is perfect for a number of different designs. For example, for the Fairy tea party (page 164), you will need to make moulds for the teacups and saucers.

1 You need two ping-pong balls. Start by cutting one of the balls neatly in half. Attach the whole ping-pong ball and one of the halves (cut side up), to a sturdy board, using a glue gun or craft glue. The whole ball should have its seam running horizontally around the middle. These will become the moulds for the teacups (Pic a).

2 Roll out a small piece of fondant icing (mixed with Tylose powder) to about 3 mm (1/8 in) thick on a surface that has been dusted with cornflour. Drape the icing over the whole ball with the cornflour surface against the ball (Pic b).

3 Trim the icing, using a small sharp knife, at the halfway mark (Pic c). This will become the teacup.

4 Lightly dust the inside of the halved ball with cornflour and fill with fondant icing (mixed with Tylose), then trim the top level, using a small sharp knife (Pic d). This will become the contents of the cup.

5 For the moulds for the saucers, knead a little Tylose into some fondant and roll it out until it is about 6 mm (1/4 in) thick. (We have used green, for contrast, but the fondant should be uncoloured.) Cut out a disc larger than the desired size for your saucers, then cut out a hole in the centre, slightly smaller than the proposed saucer. Gently press the centre of this mould to form a slope towards the centre hole. For the saucer, cut a disc of rolled fondant (mixed with Tylose)

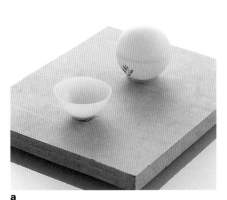

a

b

c

d

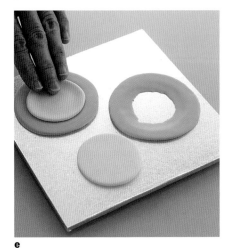

e

f

using the template. Dust the mould liberally with cornflour to absorb any moisture. Place the saucer disc into the centre of the mould and gently press to shape the edges of the saucer (Pic e).

6 Allow all the teacup and saucer pieces to dry for at least 24 hours. Once they are dry, remove the individual pieces from their moulds and assemble and glue them together as needed (Pic f).

Making a template

Making templates is an essential part of cake decorating, allowing you to cut any shape.

Choose a reference, such as a font or picture. You may need to photocopy the design to either enlarge or reduce it to the desired size to suit your cupcake. Once you have a reference, there are two basic ways to make a template.

Method A

Using a fine-tip pen and either a round template or a round cutter the same size as your cupcake icing, trace a circle (or circles) onto your artwork, so that the design is in the centre of the circle. Cover the artwork with a piece of tracing paper. Using either your hand or tape to hold the tracing paper steady, trace over the image and the circle outline, using a fine-tip pen (Pic a).

Turn the tracing paper over (to get the mirror image) and carefully trace over the previously traced design lines with a soft 2B pencil (Pic b). You do not need to trace over the circles — they are a placement guide only.

Method B

For this method you will need a lightbox, but you can improvise by using a sunny window or even a lamp under a glass-topped coffee table.

On top of the lightbox, flip your reference artwork over onto the wrong side. If you are using a window, tape the image, right side down, to the window. Because of the light source, you will be able to see the outline clearly in mirror image.

Place the tracing paper over the reversed image and, using a pen, trace the circles to define the cupcake outlines. Then, using a 2B pencil, trace the design inside the circles onto the tracing paper (Pic c).

a

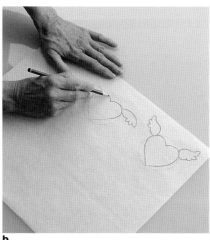

b

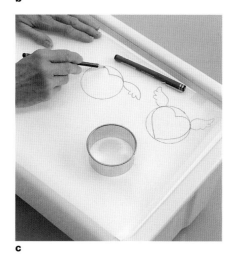

c

Transferring a template

Once you have made a template for your chosen design, you need to transfer the outline onto the icing, so you can cut it out or use it as a guide for placing decorations on the cupcake.

Place the tracing on the icing, with the mirror-image 2B pencil lines face-down on the icing itself. If the icing is soft, a light sweep across the paper with your hand is often enough to transfer the pencil outline onto the icing. If the icing is harder, trace or rub over the lines on the tracing paper with a skewer at a 45 degree angle, taking care not to dent the icing with too much pressure (Pic d).

You can now use a small sharp knife to cut accurately along the transferred lines or use them as a guide to place cut-out decorations.

Tip

If you plan to use your templates repeatedly, you can make them more permanent by tracing the outlines onto waxy cardboard and cutting them out. By keeping your templates and template boards, you can amass a library and save time in the future.

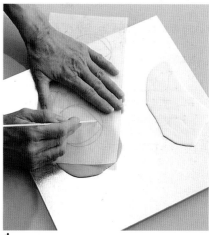

d

Templates for mosaics

1 Choose a picture — either a template from this book or a simple picture, such as a cartoon or image from a child's colouring book. These are easier to make and they look good with blocks of plain colour. You can alter the shape of the border in any way you wish but obviously, a square or rectangle grid is easiest to reproduce.

2 Now, make the cupcake template. This is very easy. Start with a fine-tip pen and a sheet of tracing paper, large enough to accommodate the whole mosaic design. Using a cupcake circle cutter the same size as the top of each cupcake, draw cupcake circles on the paper in a grid that will accommodate the entire picture, including any outline or borders that the picture may have (Pic a).

3 If the size of your chosen design needs to be altered, use a photocopier to increase or decrease it to the required size, and print it out. If you don't have a printer, trace your design onto paper, using a fine-tip pen (Pic b).

4 Turn the design face down and place the cupcake template on top of it. (The design must be face down as you need to make a mirror-image, so that it ends up being the right way round when transferred to the cupcakes.) Take both pieces of paper to a window or put them on top of a lightbox so that you can see both pictures clearly on top of each other. Using a 2B pencil, trace the original picture onto the cupcake template (Pic c). This is your completed template ready to be transferred onto your cupcakes, or to trace and cut shapes for smaller sections of your design.

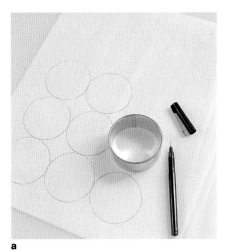

a

b

c

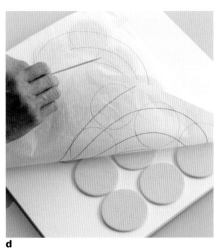

d

5 To transfer a mosaic design, place the cupcake fondant covers on the bench in a grid pattern, as in the template. Line up the circle outlines over the covers, and transfer the design, as for Transferring a template (page 221) (Pic d). With mosaics, it is better to transfer the design onto set rounds of fondant before covering the cupcakes, as the even surface makes the transferring of the design much easier.

Tip

When transferring your template to the icing, press very gently. If the icing is still soft, the design should transfer with just the pressure of your hand. If it does not, you may need a wooden skewer to trace over the lines. If you press gently, you should be able to use the same template several times. After repeated transfers, however, you may need to go over the traced lines again with a 2B pencil.

Troubleshooting

Dry icing

If your icing is dry and cracking it will be almost impossible to work with. Cracking can be the result of a number of different causes. You might be over-kneading the icing and drying it out; or the environment (air conditioning or an over-heated room) could be a factor; perhaps you are taking too long to work with the icing — you must work quickly; or you may have used too much Tylose powder. Whatever the cause, to remedy the problem, brush a little water on the icing and then knead it through. Alternatively, you can brush in a small amount of glycerine (see Glossary) and knead it through. If you are constantly suffering from dry icing, you might need to change the fondant brand you use or address the environment, such as air conditioning or heating, both of which will dry icing out.

Humidity

This is a cake decorator's worst enemy: decorations don't adhere, icing becomes soft and sticky and it's almost impossible to use. At Planet Cake, we mix sifted icing sugar into the icing a little at a time and knead it through. Another method is to mix Tylose into the icing.

Stains

If your icing is stained with cornflour, use cake-decorating alcohol applied with a soft paintbrush to remove the cornflour stains; pat dry with a tissue. If your icing is stained with chocolate, you will need to employ a more complex method. First, using a soft paintbrush, wash the stain lightly with warm, soapy water, then rinse the brush and gently wash the soap away with clean water. Pat lightly dry with a tissue and then lightly dust with cornflour using a soft brush.

Paper cases peeling

When the paper cases peel away from the sides of the cupcake, this is usually the result of humidity and is sometimes caused when they are covered with icing too quickly before being given enough time to cool. The icing traps the heat in the cupcake and the humidity makes the paper peel. There is nothing you can do about this, so remember to always allow enough cooling time for your cupcakes.

Wet icing

Wet icing is usually the result of too much colour pigment and often black, red and brown icing become 'wet' and difficult to work with. The remedy is the same as for humidity: knead sifted icing sugar into the icing.

Cupcakes cooking unevenly

This is probably a result of your oven not cooking at an even temperature. All ovens are different; they can also have hot and cold spots. For example, cupcakes at the back of the oven may not bake as well as those at the front. We recommend baking a maximum of 24 cupcakes in the oven at any one time. If you need to move the cupcakes around to compensate for hot/cold spots, wait 15 minutes after first putting them in before opening the door again to move them.

Cupcakes sinking

Do not disturb your cupcakes in the first 15 minutes of baking; this is their period to become structurally sound. If you open the oven door in the first 15 minutes, or take the cupcakes out of the oven prematurely, they may sink.

Cupcakes too full

Only fill the paper cases two-thirds full with mix to avoid spilling and cupcake collapse. If this has happened, you can, however, trim off the worst of the excess before covering with ganache.

Cupcakes cracking

Cupcakes can crack because the oven is too hot: the mixture is being cooked too quickly and it is being forced out the top like lava instead of baking evenly. Reduce the temperature of the oven by 10°C (50°F) and see if this makes a difference.

Sweaty cupcakes

Shiny sweaty cupcakes are the result of keeping the cupcakes in a closed container; even a closed cake box can make them sweat and the icing will become shiny and sticky. Be sure to store your cupcakes with the lid off until they need to travel, but keep a cloth over the top to prevent colour fading.

Ganache separating

Ganache separates when the cream is not mixed with the chocolate immediately: leaving the cream on top of the chocolate without emulsifying will cause the chocolate to separate. If this happens, whisk the mixture vigorously, put it in the fridge for 10 minutes to cool a little, then stir with a whisk again.

Lumpy ganache

If your ganache is lumpy, it is perhaps because you have not mixed the chocolate with the cream thoroughly or the chocolate hasn't completely melted. Give it another good stir and if this doesn't work reheat it over a saucepan of simmering water or with short bursts in the microwave until the chocolate melts. Stir well.

Templates

Pulsating hearts

enlarge by 125%

Templates

Go dog, go!

enlarge by 125%

Templates

Mix-n-match Betty Sue

enlarge by 125%

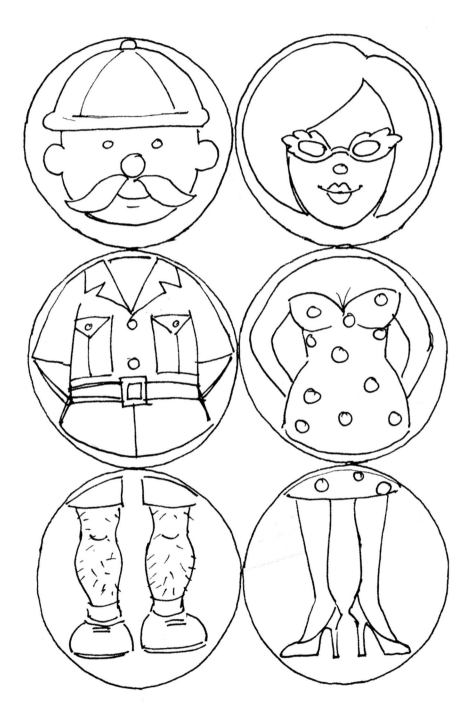

Templates

Rainbow dragon

enlarge by 133%

Templates

Zodiac

actual size

Glossary

Airbrush colours
Colours made specifically for use in an airbrush machine. Do not use colour paste for airbrushing as it will damage your machine. There is a fabulous array of airbrush colours available and these can be diluted to the desired strength with cake-decorating alcohol.

Airbrushing
A technique in which edible liquid paints are sprayed onto a cake through a fine needle tip, using compressed air, allowing for shading, stencilling and other subtle colour effects, unobtainable using a paintbrush. The paint is applied using an airbrush machine, which can be purchased at speciality cooking stores or websites.

Balling tool
This long plastic stick has a different-sized ball at either end. Use it to make round indents, such as eye sockets, and smooth curves in modelling, or to shape flower petals. They are available in different sizes.

Cake boards
Usually made from masonite and covered in gold or silver paper, cake boards are available from cake-decorating supply shops. Use them to display your cupcakes, especially the Mosaic designs.

Cake-decorating alcohol
This contains 5 per cent rose essence and is used to mix with colour paste or colour liquid for painting. It is also used for removing icing stains. Vodka can be used as a substitute.

Cornflour
Also known as cornstarch, cornflour is the starch of the maize grain. It is used in cake decorating for dusting work surfaces when rolling out the icing. It is better to use than icing sugar when rolling icing. Use sparingly as it can dry the icing out.

Couverture
Couverture is a natural, sweet chocolate containing no added fats other than cocoa butter. It is used for dipping, moulding, coating and, most importantly, for ganache making. Not to be confused with confectionery chocolate or compound chocolate, couverture is a very high-quality chocolate that contains extra cocoa butter and is usually sold in the form of buttons. The higher percentage of cocoa butter, combined with the processing, gives the chocolate more sheen, a firmer 'snap' when broken, and a creamy mellow flavour. We use a couverture chocolate with about 44–63 per cent cocoa content. This is a mid-range couverture chocolate, a little superior to what you would normally find in a supermarket. It is available from cake-decorating supply stores or speciality cooking stores, although you can sometimes find it in large supermarkets.

Cutters
Available in different sizes and shapes — such as rounds, flowers and hearts — cutters often come in sets, in plastic or stainless steel. For covering cupcakes, you need a round cutter that is the same size as the top of the cupcakes, as well as one that is one size larger; a full set of round cutters is invaluable.

Edible glitter
Available in an array of colours from cake-decorating supply stores. Apply edible glitter with water or piping gel.

Flexi-smoother
A flexi-smoother is a Planet Cake DIY invention. We use either unused X-ray film (which can be hard to get) or a thin plastic, such as acetate, computer film or the plastic used for flexible display folders (the ones with the plastic sleeves inside). Cut the plastic to a rectangle, a little larger than the palm of your hand. Round the edges using scissors, then disinfect the plastic and hey presto!

Use the flexi-smoother to buff and polish the icing helping you create razor-sharp edges and very smooth surfaces. The flexi-smoother is flexible so you can manipulate it with your hand to navigate the icing of shaped and complex cakes to eliminate all the air bubbles and bumps in the icing, resulting in a smooth, perfect and professional-looking icing finish.

Florist's tape
Used to cover wire for decorations.

Fondant icing
Fondant is a dough-like icing that can be rolled out, then cut out to cover cakes. It is used to cover both large cakes and cupcakes. In its ready-made form, it is also called RTR (ready-to-roll), plastic icing and sugar paste. The basic ingredient of fondant is icing sugar, with the addition of gelatine, liquid glucose and glycerine to provide a malleable, sweet paste. Most ready-made fondant comes in white or ivory and can be tinted to any colour of the rainbow.

Fondant gives cakes a beautiful, porcelain-like surface that can be painted, piped onto, cut out or stamped — the possibilities are virtually endless. Fondant is also used to 'model' and cut 3D shapes for decoration. Good-quality ready-made fondant is costly, but worth the investment. You will need to experiment with different brands to find the one that suits your needs. It is available from large supermarkets and cake-decorating supply stores.

Food or icing colours
Colour paste is the most concentrated of food colours. Mix it into fondant icing or thin it with cake-decorating alcohol to paint with. Liquid colouring is similar, but less intense.

Frilling tool

Part of a set called 'modelling tools', this tool is named because it is used to 'frill' soft surfaces, but it is probably the most versatile tool in the box, and is the one we use on almost every cake in this book, to score lines, indent facial features, mark textured surfaces for fur, hair, and so on.

Ganache

In its simplest form, ganache is equal parts chocolate and cream. Ganache can be made with dark, milk or white chocolate, or with a combination of all three. We use it to give a smooth and even surface to a cupcake before covering it with fondant icing.

Glue

To fix decorations or sections of icing to the top of cupcakes, simply add a dab of water. Use this 'adhesive' to attach the components as you would use glue, taking care not to get things too wet. You can also use syrup or piping gel for extra hold.

Glycerine

A colourless, odourless, syrupy liquid made from fats and oils and used to retain moisture and add sweetness to foods. Stir it into icing to restore consistency or use to soften fondant or royal icing. Can be used to soften dried icing colours and when making rolled fondant. It's available from chemists and cake-decorating supply stores.

Painting

Mix edible colour paste or liquid colour with cake-decorating alcohol, then paint onto fondant-covered cakes with a fine artist's brush.

Palette knife

Usually a handled flat knife with a bend (crank) in the blade, often called cranked palette knife. It is used to spread and smooth ganache onto cakes and cupcakes.

Pasta machine

Also called a pasta maker, it is used, as the name suggests, for making home-made pasta, but it's also brilliant for rolling out icing, as it provides a consistent thickness and rolls the icing perfectly.

Piping gel

Also known as piping jelly, this clear, sticky gel becomes fluid when warmed. It maintains a shiny wet look when set, so is used to give a shine to eyes, tongues and 'liquids'. It can be coloured with colour paste. It is also used for attaching icing decorations.

Piping tips and coupler

The size and shape of the opening on a piping tip determines the type of decoration a tip will produce, although with royal icing, we almost always use the round tips (and very occasionally, a star tip). Round piping tips are used to make dots and outlines, as well as writing and figure piping.

The coupler sits between a material piping bag and piping tip. You can then screw the piping tip onto the coupler and easily change between different sizes and shapes without changing the piping bag.

Petal and lustre dusts

Also available in pearl and sparkle and lustre finishes, these dusts can be mixed with cake-decorating alcohol to give a metallic lustre to decorations. Red and/or pink petal dust can be brushed on dry to give cheeks a rosy glow.

Pre-coloured icing

To make red or black icing, you will need pre-coloured icing. Available from cake-decorating supply stores. The advantage of pre-coloured icing is the intensity of the colour pigment.

Rolling pins

A small rolling pin is ideal for small projects and rolling out small pieces of icing. You can buy a fancy one from a cake-decorating supply store, but the most prized small rolling pins at Planet Cake are those found in children's baking sets.

We also use large rolling pins to roll out icing. The types available are: without handles, with integral handles or, our favourite, with handles that are attached to a central rod in the roller. Rolling pins, whether made from wood, marble or silicon, should have absolutely smooth surfaces, with no dints or marks that will transfer to your icing.

Royal icing

A mixture of egg white (or albumen) and icing sugar with a little lemon juice or vinegar, royal icing is used for piping decorations onto cupcakes. It dries hard and can be coloured with edible food colour. You can buy instant royal icing powder where you just have to add water, or you can make your own.

Syrup or soaking syrup

A mixture of boiled water and jam in the ratio of 1:1; used to moisten surfaces of cut cakes or between the ganache and icing covering to help adhere the icing. It can be flavoured with alcohol.

Tylose powder

If mixed into rolled fondant, marzipan or royal icing, this non-toxic chemical — carboxymethylcellulose (CMC) — forms a strong modelling paste that dries hard. Tylose powder can also be mixed with water to make thick, strong edible glue.

White-white colour paste

This colour paste is an intense white and is used for whitening icings, especially those that contain butter. We use it mainly to add white highlights to eyes.

Wire

Available from cake-decorating stores, florist's wire is used for adding support to 3D icing elements and for helping to attach them to the cupcake. It comes in several different thicknesses (called gauges). We use mostly 22-gauge wire. When making cupcakes for children, it is better to use dried spaghetti.

Index